MY CHILD

"The Quick Fix?"

One Day At A Time

C.S. Harrison

CSR Publishing
HOUSTON

MY CHILD

Copyright © 2013 by CSR Publishing

Printed in the United States of America

All rights reserved. No part of this book may be reproduced in any form, except for the inclusion of brief quotations in review, without the expressed written consent from the author and/or publisher.

LIBRARY OF CONGRESS
2013-93536

CSR Publishing
4409 Almeda Road
Houston, Texas 77004

www.mychildthebook.com

Some names and identifying details have been changed to protect the privacy of individuals.

DEDICATION

This book is dedicated to my loving mother, Shirley Harrison, who set me on a path to experience life with compassion, care and a thirst for knowledge.

My Child

TABLE OF CONTENTS

CHAPTER ONE
The Apple Does Not Fall Far From the Tree

CHAPTER TWO
Understanding the Brain

CHAPTER THREE
An Apple a Day Keeps the Doctor Away

CHAPTER FOUR
Play

CHAPTER FIVE
Love Hurts Sometimes

CHAPTER SIX
It Takes a Village to Raise a Child

CHAPTER SEVEN
More Unites Us Than Divides Us

CHAPTER EIGHT
Organizational Learning

CHAPTER NINE
At First You Don't Succeed Try, Try Again

CHAPTER TEN
Wonder Years

CHAPTER ELEVEN
Love Me for Me

CHAPTER TWELVE
LOVE. FAITH. HOPE.

INTRODUCTION

"Change will not come if we wait for some other person or some other time. We are the ones we've been waiting for. We are the change that we seek." ~ Barack Obama

We live in a world where labels, programs, and studies place our children in categories. I believe every child is born with the same capacity and innate ability to achieve excellence; regardless of race, gender, economic or social background. Hence -- my quest to understand the development of children. From my research and observations, I'm convinced there are four components collectively working in balance attempting to establish the best route in the growth and progress of our children. Education, behavior control, cultural exposure, and health -- equally monitored and understood -- provide opportunity.

I was raised in a single-family setting after my parents divorced. It was my mother who established the foundation for my success. She created structure and discipline in our home, and taught me the value of family and meaningful relationships. My mother understood the importance of being multi-talented. She saw and seized opportunity when there seemed to be none....and had the ability to adjust, adapt, and advance. I learned these attributes from her and thank her for raising me into the man, and father, I am today.

As humans, we have the capability to self-regulate our behavior. This includes: developing good eating habits, engaging in physical activity, maintaining adequate sleep, and gaining exposure to social and cultural experiences. As parents we must practice self-restraint and dedication in our efforts to teach our kids right from wrong. Now that I have children, I ask myself what I want for them. I wonder how to maximize their potential without too much or too little pressure, or when I should expect certain goals and behaviors to be met. I know parenting can be the hardest, but, most rewarding job we have.

While on my quest to understand the psychological and scientific reasoning that contribute to the development of our children, I asked myself a lot of the same questions you are now asking yourself. What do I ultimately want for my child? How can I best raise him or her to make the right decisions? And so forth. My hope is that the presentation of this material, the supporting data, and my personal experiences better prepares you to make the best possible decisions for you and your family.

CHAPTER ONE

THE APPLE DOESN'T FALL FAR FROM THE TREE

"A child only educated at school is an uneducated child."
~ George Santayana

     Growing up in Mississippi, the state of hospitality, there were two homes that I truly cherished - my mother's in Jackson and my extended family's in Vicksburg. Both households influenced the person and father I've become... paving a path of success and establishing a solid foundation on which to base my own parenting skills. While my childhood was not perfect, the lessons I learned from my many trials and tribulations have been the stepping stones to my personal and professional life. My grandmother, Lubertha, was the matriarch of the family. She raised her thirteen children to be hardworking, self-disciplined, God fearing individuals. Respected for her guidance, advice, and wisdom she provided them, they sought the same for her thirty-seven grandchildren. And for twenty years, this became her life's work at Head Start, a program that ensures vulnerable children and families have access to the support they need in order for children to succeed.

     Perhaps it was her upbringing that made her successful in raising her kids and in her career. My grandmother built upon the techniques of my great-grandmother, Dora. Using the bible as her primary resource—since there was limited information during the 1930s; my great-grandmother used biblical principles to raise good, productive people.

Shirley, my mother was a young country woman. Vibrant and full of energy, she was eager to trade the country life for a more exciting one in the city of Jackson to attend college. Even though her new life was only thirty minutes away, to her it felt like traveling across America. She was leaving a pretty secure life. But, she was ready to start her own adventure. And the advice she received from her mother, *"Be smart and take care of yourself,"* would serve her well.   At college, my mother was exposed to a whole new world of information. The foundation and lessons my grandmother provided, helped her differentiate between the people who would be negative influences and those who had her best interest in mind. A beautiful, intelligent, young lady, it was no wonder my father, Henry III, found her attractive. He was born in Kansas, but raised in Chicago. Career-driven and focused, are two key words that describe him. You see, he grew up in a fast-paced environment and was taught at an early age *one needed to make his mark on society*. His father, Henry II, represented the American Federation of Labor and Congress of Industrial Organizations (AFL-CIO) in Chicago and trained him as if he were one of the men in the teamsters' organizations. So, when he met my mother, he was overwhelmed by what he considered a complexity of attributes... while admiring the simplicity of what made her happy. Eventually the two were married. But, after three years, my father started placing his career before his family which led to their divorce. Imagine me, a three year old child trying to comprehend why his father was leaving. With my words pleading and my heart saddened *"Please don't leave daddy, I will be a good boy."* Leaving my mother, forced to raise two children alone, scared and unprepared. But, her survival instincts kicked in and luckily, she was able to reach out to her family for help. Her family was her support system... no matter what happened they were there to help. While they openly gave her information about the things they knew, she wondered when and where to seek information about the things her family was not knowledgeable about. At that time, there was no internet... just people, newspapers, television, and books.

Nearly five years after the divorce, my mother started changing. Some of her friends were positive influences...others, it turned out, were negative on all of us. However; there were lessons to be learned in each interaction. Seeing that my mother's ambitions were spiraling into the abyss, my grandmother stepped in to offer sound advice, *"If you want to raise good kids, you have to stay out of the streets."* She also said, *"You don't have to teach a child the wrong things in life, the world will teach them that. Your job as a parent is to sift through the bad...look for the good."*.... *"Explain why and when things go wrong, and the consequences that follow."* My mother took my grandmother's advice. She knew she would have to rely on others to help care for my sister, Erinn and I, so she created a plan of action – choosing to seek out information before anything could go terribly wrong. She worked diligently every day to balance our lives by ensuring we got adequate sleep, learned appropriate and responsible behavior, gained healthy eating habits, and made sure we exercised our minds and bodies. As with many parents during that time, my mother wasn't educated in the neuroscience behind cultural exposure, healthy eating habits, and behavioral control. But, she intuitively recognized many of the factors and techniques modern parenting books now preach, and knew she wanted her children to be educated, healthy, well behaved, and diverse.

In my teenage years, I saw my mom in many different roles. She expended every effort to model the behavior she expected from us. She embodied the roles of educator, disciplinarian, and nurturer. She always demonstrated the educator. The wise old saying *"Do as I do, not as I say,"* comes to mind – she certainly led by example. "The disciplinarian"... my sister and I had to keep up with our obligations -- no ands, if, or buts, they needed to be done. Lastly "the nurturer"... I remember her telling us, *"Smile and you may make someone's day better."* At times I did think of her as too strict though. Her unpredictability along with interchanging multiple roles was profound. Now that I am a parent, I understand why.

Many years later, while in the delivery room with my wife, watching my son Sloan enter this world, flashes of my life came to the forefront. Feeling overjoyed with excitement, I suddenly realized I wanted and needed to be a strong father figure for him and asked myself the all-important questions: *What do I want for my child? Where will I gather information? What is my plan of action to achieve the goals I have set?* In that moment, I truly understood the questions and decisions my mother and grandmother were faced with. When my son was born... into a world of manipulation, false hopes, and empty promises... I wanted to make sure he would be surrounded by people who truly had his best interest in mind.

Parenting can be overwhelming. *So, where do we start? How should we raise our children? Do we replicate our parents' methods? Do we revise those methods based on social changes? Do we start over with what we believe to be correct?* I believe we must do all of the above. In trying to figure out the answers to my own personal questions, can a template be formed for all children? Through years of different professions as a teacher, father, and scientist, I wondered if a system could be created. To help parents solve some basic scenarios along the path to success.

Another question is, "Does our lifestyle, the people we associate with, and who we are, influence our judgments when parenting?" In some instances yes, in others no... Children are less likely to do things they aren't aware of, so we must expose them to positive, healthy options. One of the best examples is food... children are less likely to crave candy bars and fast food if they are given in moderation. But, if you frequently introduce them to healthy foods, they'll pick and choose the foods they enjoy most. If your children make a habit of eating healthy food options, it could help them develop, maintain, and enjoy good health overall. We often take for granted our status of well-being. Health can be a tricky obstacle depending on family history. Knowing the facts and staying informed allows us to be proactive.

Social behavior at times is dictated by our peers and environment. While we cannot always have complete control over the social influences to which our children are exposed; guiding their curiosity is fostered by creating a trusting relationship with your child. If guidance is not over-reached, then children will be able to effectively choose healthy relationships and make positive choices. Children can be influenced to seek the things they know and don't know, especially when they become older. Providing solid guidance can help them avoid the pitfalls such as drug use and addiction. While developing these relationships, we need to remember trust is the key.

Educational standards can definitely be set regardless of the environment you live in. We hear constantly the disparities between families of wealthy, middle and low income families. As we raise our children, we must ask ourselves, *Are we providing them too few or too many options? Are they educated enough to make the right choices? Is there a limit on what will be tolerated?* All these questions are vital. We should expose our kids to different options... at the same time; we need to be cautious of the options the world offers to them. Deciding when and how to raise our children is often taken for granted. Genetics and environmental factors influence a child at the moment of conception. We should never wait until birth to begin asking important questions about childrearing. Create a plan that indicates what you aspire for your children to become and how you plan to help them get there. But, recognize that they may fall short or exceed your expectations.

As parents, we strive to provide opportunities for our children to become successful... we also hope they're happy. However, what success and happiness means will differ from child to child. As a parent there will be times you will feel alone and not possess the strength to move forward... maybe even feel like everything is going wrong. This is okay. Ask for help from educators, family members, and friends. Encouraging people will be there to help you, but you must ask for that help. Now and again we need the help of someone more knowledgeable than ourselves. Support from the people who care for you and your child makes raising your child much easier. Parenting is not something you have to do alone and master in a day's time. Once everyone around you sings a song of excellence, responsibility, and respect, children have no choice but to aspire for greatness. When they work hard to achieve their goals they feel a sense of meaning and personal fulfillment. In my family, we look to a higher power to help us to stay strong and persevere. We realized that sometimes the human capacity limits us at times. We all need help encouraging ourselves, finding that inner power to overcome. Faith has helped us through many obstacles, and I believe everyone needs someone, whether it is a spiritual figure or a person they trust, to turn to in times of struggle.

Parenting is a JOB and often before starting a new job, we educate ourselves on duties we feel we need to know before day one of actually working. This helps us feel more confident. I will admit I was not always confident in my parenting and teaching abilities. Being educated and having a strong background in the science field, I understood things to be black or white, right or wrong, and that was the way I was raised. Either I did what my parents and their support system said, or I suffered the consequences. In a world with so many variations of color and opportunity, there are not always clear and direct answers to the concerns and problems that we face today. I realize there is not one right way to raise a child and that many solutions are situational.

We often hear the quote, *"Your child is a reflection of you; he gets it honest."* While we influence who our children become, there are also many outside factors that influence them. In science, this is referred to as the nature vs. nurture debate. However modern science proves that a child's success is not based solely on genetic or environmental factors, but rather a combination of both. Children often mimic what their parents do. My mother realized this very early on and made it her goal to be a positive role model... now, that I am a father, that's my goal too. She told us to work hard and take responsibility for our actions. She led by example and we followed.

In my own life, I see the same type of behavior with my son. After a long day of work, I sat down and watched my son, Sloan, play on the carpet with his toys. He paused for a minute... which gave me a clue he was distracted by something. Since, we were in full-fledged potty training mode and that pause meant *"Take me to the potty".* Before I could move, my wife, Tina, jumped up calling out and pointing in the direction of the bathroom. *"Sloan, let's go to the potty!"* she exclaimed. As I watched, he mimicked her exact gesture and he exclaimed, *"Go to the potty!"* This interaction happened a few times until she took his hand and started leading him to *"the potty"*.

Meantime, I had my head hidden behind a pillow laughing at the sight of the scene unfolding in front of me. My wife then turned to me and said, *"Chris, don't laugh it's not funny,"* after which she took him to the potty, and the mission was a success. This display of Sloan mimicking his mother's techniques made me more aware of how much attention he pays to what we say *and* how we behave. After this, I definitely had become more aware of my actions around him.

Modern society has made it more common for us to outsource the raising of our kids. Sometimes the television and internet becomes a child's *nanny*. These vices can introduce a variety of messages and images that can be difficult for parents, to monitor. Sometimes adults outsource their kids to other adults. Whether it is family members, friends, schools, or extracurricular programs, it is important that we, as parents, thoroughly know and understand who is caring for our children and what messages they are providing to our children.

Programs that are created and dedicated to helping children succeed can help strengthen their character, and alter negative messages and behaviors they may be experiencing. In addition, these programs can provide parents with access to information they may otherwise have had access. For instance, educators are often the first to recognize when a child is having trouble learning and can help identify ways for the school and parents to work together to improve the child's ability to succeed. Parents must be willing to accept this knowledge and use it in order for it to be beneficial. Often though, the tone and delivery of information by an educator may be misinterpreted and leaves the person receiving the information feeling belittled and more like a child being scorned than a responsible parent. Adults often ask for help, but once they are given advice, depending on the delivery they may reject the person's suggestions.

I remember an instance when I visited Houston's Smith

Public Library and a baby began crying uncontrollably in his mother's arms, while she was tending to an elderly relative. The young woman appeared to be overwhelmed. The relative walked with a cane in one hand as he held onto one of her hands with the other. Once at his destination, she took her baby, (who at this point was screaming) to the restroom. I and others overheard the sounds of her spanking the child, which in turn caused him to yell and scream even louder. Immediately, I went over and asked her to stop. The woman was surprised. But I asked if I could help her understand why her son was crying like that. When I asked if the child was hungry, she became defensive. *"Of course, I fed my child. I am not a bad parent,"* she said. I softened my tone to try and build a rapport with her and as she became more comfortable, I was able to continue asking questions. After a few minutes of the child listening to my soothing tone, I began to notice he was possibly just tired as he was rubbing his eyes. I asked the mother if she had a pacifier, she didn't. So, I asked her if she had a sippy cup, she did. I held onto the child, while she ran out to get it from her car. As her son begins to calm down from the cool drink of water, I returned her son to her. I mentioned it was natural for him to be resistant to falling asleep. *"Try laying his head on your shoulder-- while rubbing his back, speak to him calmly."* I explained *"This will help relax him"* and he fell asleep almost immediately. Because of my experience in early childhood development, I helped the mother understand that when children do not have the ability to use words, they find other ways to show what they need and want. As an educator, I know children act out in different ways to get their points of view across. While some of this gets misinterpreted as whining or misbehaving, there may be other underlying reasons. We, as parents, should step back, listen, and then decide how to best approach the situation.

  Throughout my years of working in early childhood development, and daily interactions with people from various walks of life; each person has a personal perspective of what they consider to be important, when it comes to raising kids. As a parent, what do you consider important?

CHAPTER TWO
UNDERSTANDING THE BRAIN

"The human brain is a most unusual instrument of elegant and as yet unknown capacity." ~ Stuart Seaton

The brain is possibly, the most misunderstood, but most valued piece of equipment the human body possesses. During my research to fully understand the essentials for early development in children, I ran across a publication from the National Research Council and Institute of Medicine entitled *From Neurons to Neighborhoods* which explains children's processing mechanisms.

The committee that contributed to this collaboration ranged from an extensive academic analysis of people from Stanford University Department of Pediatrics to UC Berkeley's Department of Economics to the University of Washington's Department of Multicultural Education along with others. Their research identifies ten principles to "frame understanding of the nature of early human development."

1. Human development is shaped by a dynamic and continuous interaction between biology and experience.
2. Culture influences every aspect of human development and is reflected in childrearing beliefs and practices designed to promote healthy adaptation.

3. The growth of self-regulation is a cornerstone of early childhood development that cuts across all domains of behavior.
4. Children are active participants in their own development, reflecting the intrinsic human drive to explore and master one's environment.
5. Human relationships, and the effects of relationships on relationships, are the building blocks of healthy development.
6. The broad range of individual differences among young children often makes it difficult to distinguish normal variations and maturational delays from transient disorders and persistent impairments.
7. The development of children unfolds along individual pathways whose trajectories are characterized by continuities and discontinuities, as well as by a series of significant transitions.
8. Human development is shaped by the ongoing interplay among sources of vulnerability and sources of resilience.
9. The timing of early experiences can matter, but, more often than not, the developing child remains vulnerable to risks and open to protective influences throughout the early years of life and into adulthood.
10. The course of development can be altered in early childhood by effective interventions that change the balance between risk and protection, thereby shifting the odds in favor of more adaptive outcomes.

Then, there's what their committee concluded and recommended which are

1. All children are born wired for feelings and ready to learn.
2. Early environments matter and nurturing relationships are essential.
3. Society is changing and the needs of young children are not being addressed.

Interactions among early childhood science, policy, and practice are problematic and demand dramatic rethinking.

My sister, Erinn, a woman full of character with a sincere love for children, always wanted thirteen kids like our grandmother. She played with dolls, combing their hair, pretending they were her own. Years later her dreams would come true. January 2005, Erinn's Heart Early Learning Academy opened its doors. That first year involved a lot of perseverance, dedication and faith. Both of us made sacrifices to build her dream into reality. Early Childhood Education, an industry many consider a critical stage in human development, had two new visionaries attempting to save America's children. Erinn had minimal training in educating, preparing, or optimizing children's development. I had no experience running a small business; therefore we were both in over our heads. But then again we were in it for the long haul.

The first few months were pretty dismal financially. The notion that Erinn's Heart would be an instant success was wishful thinking. Erinn would contact me at work to update me on the slow progress. In the back of my mind, I had my own doubts. *Are we in over our heads*? Nobody in our family owned their own business or ran a school. *"What was I thinking?"* Several months followed, Erinn's pregnancy was in its 2nd trimester. And in June, I flew to Columbus, Ohio to attend my college roommate's wedding. Moments before the ceremony, Erinn calls me, tells me she doesn't believe we will make it. In response, I reassured her we would be okay. *"We have to keep learning everyday"* I would tell her. *"We have to be patient, we will have more children than you can imagine."* While standing along with the other groomsmen, thoughts were running rampant in my mind.

On the flight back from Ohio, I returned to the memories of our childhood together. I would recall the times that she ran behind me wanting to follow me everywhere and to become everything I set out to be. She was my baby sister, and I would not allow any obstacles to prevent her from achieving her dreams. That trip gave me time to reflect on my own personal life which translated into Erinn's Heart. We surely didn't want to give children the minimum; we wanted to provide learning as if they were our own. Enrollment began to increase, children were coming from everywhere. Now we had a good problem. The space we leased now became too small to facilitate all the kids that were coming. January 2006, we moved into a larger facility that accommodated three times the capacity of our previous building. Each day was a constant emotional rollercoaster. Our mission was to improve as much as possible each day, but each day parents wanted something different. The unpredictability of the business helped us develop thick layers of skin. We were well on our way again, so we thought; only later to have complacency slow us down. We had gotten too comfortable.

In the fall of 2008 Erinn's Heart collaborated with Young Learners Academy (YLS), a non-profit organization that provides childcare centers with degreed teachers. YLS introduced the classroom setting that showcased learning through play. Circle time demonstrated the equivalent of instructional time in a higher level classroom. YLS's classroom setting displayed the mental capacity of young children's ability to be engaged in various activities. YLS highlighted on the social development of children, but academically we thought more could be achieved. Even though we were thankful for everything that YLS provided. We believed that the children were just achieving the basic knowledge, but didn't truly challenge the full capacity of their abilities. The children often gave signals of boredom and complacency. "Do we allow brilliant minds eager for more information to be idle?" Our answer was definitely "No". The next question became "With increased learning, could they retain the material for usage later?" We had to try. Our own case studies were being conceived.

The summer of 2009 was a turning point in my life; I decided to resign from my position at Bioassay Laboratories. For nine and a half years, I worked tirelessly for someone else's gain. Now I wanted to commit myself totally to my own business. Not having any formal training in the education field, my approach was to take all the methods I saw effective. In our normal routine, naptime was approximately 2 hours. The older children who would be entering Kindergarten the following year only slept 45 minutes to an hour. I chose to take one student, Everett, and use the extra hour to experiment with different educational material. We began working with first grade material. Each day during nap time, I would explain that material. He would process the information so rapidly it was astonishing. Everett's desire to learn more gave me inspiration. The work increased in difficulty, I felt that he was taking in lots of information. While reviewing his prior work; his responses to the problems were accurate. The time it took to retrieve the answers was the only difference. The summer ended. Everett went on to kindergarten, and I began my first semester as an official teacher. I thought, *"A teacher!! HUH? Me?* My life's plan did not notify me about this adventure. My mind was going haywire, and I finally resolved; "*What the heck...I guess? LET'S DO IT!!*

    Pre-K4... I'm sure they were as puzzled as I was. My motto for the class "Learn First, Play Later", this was my foundation. It sent their minds into a midst of confusion. I needed them to understand the importance of completing tasks, then playing once they were finished. My mother's teaching of *"There is a time and place for everything"* jumped into my mind. She was preparing me for life's lessons; that everything won't be fun and games. There will be times when life demands focus. The kids were receptive to the guidelines that were set. The children eager for more knowledge set a great example for others to be curious. I initiated open discussion which was vital for changing the children's attitudes about new ideas. Of course not all were as inquisitive, there were some that were more disruptive which easily took the class off focus. In an effort to keep the atmosphere productive and enjoyable, there were times I asked the children to remove themselves from the group. Resorting to my chemistry methodology, I would look at that scenario as "extracting the contaminate", once we did that, then we were back on track.

So, I ask myself "Do most of the world's issues we face today actually begin during the early years? What happened to the child that had such a bright future? From infancy to adolescence, where was the ball dropped?" The Center on The Developing Child at Harvard University identifies three core concepts that provide the foundation in early childhood development. The first "Serve & Return Interaction Shapes Brain Circuitry"; the second "Experiences Build Brain Architecture" and the third, "Toxic Stress Derails Healthy Development";

> "The basic architecture of the brain is constructed through a process that begins early in life and continues into adulthood. Simpler circuits come first and more complex brain circuits build on them later. Together they shape the quality of brain architecture and establish either sturdy or a fragile foundation for all of the learning, health and behavior that follow. Neurons send electric signals to communicate. Circuits and connections are formed from repeated use the environment dictates which circuits are used. The ones that are used more are strongest and become more permanent. The ones that fade away are through a process called pruning. Through repeated use motor skills, language, visual, behavioral control, memory, and emotion become more efficient. While they originate in specific areas of the brain they are interconnected you cannot have one skill without the other. The same as building the foundation of a house."

Now I needed to know what these individual skills produced specifically and how to maximize each. First, *Memory,* the ability for information to be encoded, stored and retrieved. *Encoding* being the initial receiving and processing of shared material. Second, the capability of *Storage,* which consists of a lasting record of the encoded data. Finally, *Retrieval,* the ability to recall stored information during a process or indication. *Emotion* is a complex psycho-physiological experience of an individual's state of mind when interacting with internal and external influences. *Motor Skills* are a learned sequence of movements that combine to produce a smooth, efficient action in order to master a particular task. *Behavior* refers to the actions and mannerisms made by the human body in conjunction with its environment. *Visual system* enables the human body to process and interpret information and surroundings from the effects of visible light reaching the eye. *Language* refers to human capacity for acquiring and using complex systems of communication. Now it began to make a little more sense why my students were performing so well in specific areas. Each child's environment presented an opportunity for one or more of these skills to be heightened. Still there was no clarification why some continued to progress and others wavered. Once again I was faced with another question "Are their external environments consistent with the interactions they receive at school and home?

Stress, a highly critical component of the human well-being, has influenced the way specific responses occur. Harvard University's Center on The Developing Child has presented three responses in the way the body delivers stress.

> *"Positive stress response* is a normal and essential part of healthy development, characterized by brief increases in heart rate and mild elevations in hormone levels. Some situations that might trigger a positive stress response are the first day with a new caregiver or receiving an injected immunization."

> *"Tolerable stress response* activates the body's alert systems to a greater degree as a result of more severe, longer-lasting difficulties, such as the loss of a loved one, a natural disaster, or a frightening injury. If the activation is time-limited and buffered by relationships with adults who help the child adapt, the brain and other organs recover from what might otherwise be damaging effects."

> "*Toxic stress response* can occur when a child experiences strong, frequent, and/or prolonged adversity—such as physical or emotional abuse, chronic neglect, caregiver substance abuse or mental illness, exposure to violence, and/or the accumulated burdens of family economic hardship—without adequate adult support. This kind of prolonged activation of the stress response systems can disrupt the development of brain architecture and other organ systems, and increase the risk for stress-related disease and cognitive impairment, well into the adult years."

In May 2008, my previous employer felt necessary improvement was needed in my social and communication skills. Not that I thought they were inefficient, but they "could" be improved. In awe, that they viewed my skills as inadequate made me feel useless in presenting information in a proper way. And in order to keep my job, I was told by my C.E.O. that I needed to take a class; "Gaining Control of Ourselves" by George Anderson – the title of the training course. Anderson served as technical consultant to the movie *Anger Management*. Upon entering the class, I was apprehensive and unsure of what to expect. I have to admit, the course made me aware of my emotional state which influenced my ability to communicate with others.

In the course, first I had to identify my behavior while interacting with others. Was I passive, passive-aggressive, assertive, or aggressive? Understanding EI or Emotional Intelligence consisted of four principles.

- The first, being *Self-Awareness* "Reading one's own emotions and recognizing their impact. Knowing one's strengths and limits; with a sense of one's self worth and capabilities." I thought my emotions were appropriate. But, since they did not share my frustrations or happiness, people had no idea how to measure my feelings about different things that mattered to me.

- Second, *Self-Control,* "Keeping disruptive emotions and impulses under control, flexibly adapting to changing situations or new obstacles, and the drive to perform to meet personal standards." Because of my stubbornness, I was not readily open to receiving advice to improve my weaknesses.
- Third, *Social-Awareness*, "Sensing other's emotion's, understanding their perspectives, and taking active interest in their concerns; recognizing and meeting the needs of others." I constantly felt it was appropriate to advise others – I assumed everyone thought as I did. In reality though, that is not the case as every person thinks differently.
- Finally, *Relationship Management*, "Resolving disagreements, utilizing partnership, cooperation, and teamwork; influence decisions and outcomes while respecting the right of others" At times I refused to cooperate with others if they did not feel as I did about any given circumstance. I could even be unresponsive to certain outcomes, if it did not satisfy my personal viewpoint.

Now becoming emotionally intelligent, depending on the setting, I could transition from passive to aggressive without knowing. Therefore, I needed to have an enhanced understanding of the behavior I exhibited -- *passive* the condition of submitting to one's superiority or superiors; *passive-aggressive* submitting to one's superiority then pressed to the tipping point where all previous encounters causing a response of uncontrollable emotions; *assertive* a confident declaration or affirmation of a statement without the need of proof; and, finally, *aggressive* is behavior that is forceful, hostile and attacking, the intention to display or increase dominance. The terms began to make sense, and for the first time I identified myself in different situations. In training courses, whenever new information was presented, I demonstrated passive behavior. When errors occurred frequently by the same people I expressed passive-aggressive behavior. In a matter of seconds my emotions went from frustrations to angers, placing me in a state of aggression. When things ran smoothly tended to be the times, I learned, I was expressing assertive behavior. The class also helped me become aware of the preeminent actions of others, and how my behavior needed to be altered to create a calm and productive atmosphere.

Until I took the training class, I was deficient in social and communication skills. As a child I suffered from shyness, feeling like an imbecile whenever I spoke. *"He's shy and thinks a lot,"* my mother would say when I was younger. Now...I know that I truly need to allow myself to open up. In communicating with my colleagues, I wasn't able to express myself the way I wanted, because I believed the solutions to some of the problems were clear. My belief was, if they possessed the same training, education, and resources, as me, then they should be able to come to the same conclusions as I did. In several instances, they did not. And in my frustrations, I would vent to my mother. Who would tell me *"All adults are not the same, people do not think the way you think."* Even though I knew this to be true, I felt that some of my colleagues were underachieving and leaving responsibility to the few employees who took their jobs seriously.

As a teacher, my students possessed these same qualities. Some of the children understood from verbal instruction and others through hands-on application. Others used their own applications before formulating their own terminology and methods, and then referred back to the initial instruction. This was the group which I persistently guided the entire day. All the children held the skills to obtain the knowledge. My patience, persistence, and perseverance had to be modified based on the individual personalities...which kept me dedicated, knowing I could make a difference.

Having been in childcare for many years, we've encountered many parents pleading for help. Phrases ranging from, *"I don't know why my infant cries so much?"* to *"I fed her, her diaper is dry, she won't calm down"* ... stating questions, giving answers, all in the same sentence. Children give subtle signs of distress, when there is something troubling them. Infants use crying because of the inability to communicate with words...but, those cries differs in volume and pitch, giving parents a warning signal. The same holds true for preteens and adolescents. I often hear, "*My son is having a difficult time adjusting to his new school, but he had no issues while attending his previous school*". Social skills and how they are used could be the difference. Asking questions like: *In which areas is my child having problems?* Could it be a question of...*Does limited exposure make my child vulnerable in certain situations and prevent them from adapting?* When kids try to explain the factors to us, as parents, it's possible we may unintentionally be altering the components. Therefore, actively listening to what they're saying and/or expressing is ever so important.

Our definition of success changes as we become older, some resulting from events and people. Not that they have to, but often do. Priorities begin to cultivate during a child's adolescence years, impacting who they ultimately want to become.

CHAPTER THREE
AN APPLE A DAY KEEPS THE DOCTOR AWAY

"Health is not valued till sickness comes"~ Thomas Fuller

As an educator, making sure my students have adequate skills is a priority. Equally important is emphasizing sleep and balanced eating habits. And at Erinn's Heart, as one of the Key Decision-Makers, these two subjects are very important for our staff to establish with our students and parents. Each day children would arrive as early as 6:30 AM sometimes appearing sleep deprived. My days were usually unpredictable as a result of sleep deprivation…so I could imagine what they faced. I realized children require more sleep, therefore teaching kids and their parents about the effects of misguided health practices seemed fundamental.

We would offer breakfast daily from 7:00 A.M. to 8:00 A.M, some would eat, others would not. Not eating breakfast was foreign to me. I recall my mother making sure we ate breakfast every day. When I did refuse it was because I was not in the mood to eat. Or, as I got older, I felt sluggish if I ate a large breakfast. Not to mention, I was also picky. If it was winter, then I would not eat cereal with cold milk. Knowing how I was, I wondered what kind of challenge it would be to get our students to eat their school meals. It was interesting to find out why some chose to eat, while others did not. Some kids wondered what certain foods were, why it was textured a certain way, others wondered why some foods even looked or tasted the way they did.

I recall an instance that caused major concern. A little girl by the name of Anna who would refuse to eat lunch, only ate the snacks her parents provided. One day we persuaded her to try some vegetables but she started vomiting. Then each day after, she started to gag herself on purpose. We spoke with her parents. However, the change was short-lived. Eventually, we started noticing her having constipation issues. We brought it to the attention of Anna's parents and asked them if she was eating at home. They explained *"Anna eats what and when she feels like it." "Wow"* I thought. My mother made us eat at least one item on our plate, and here was this little girl who could choose to eat whenever and whatever she wanted. I wondered if she was receiving too many options and how this could affect her as she becomes older. Her parents believed Anna to be going through a phase. As a parent though, I believe we must lead by example and display to our kids good eating habits. When we show our kids we are making a conscious effort to make and eat balanced meals, it shows we care about what we put in our bodies. When our kids see this in action on a daily basis at home, it helps them to develop healthy ways of living.

    I also wondered if eating issues were gender based, just because I recall having to deal more with parents of female students. There were some instances in which some of the boys did not want to eat, but overall there were more issues with girls. Granted, a lot had to do with the introduction of new foods. Kiwi is a good example. Not too many of them knew what "kiwi" was. Some did say they didn't like the taste... but, come to find out, they had never tasted it. So, my next mission was to get our students to -- at least -- taste the foods, so that if they didn't like them, they knew why. This brought back lots of childhood memories, *"There are people in the world starving and dying because they have nothing to eat,"* my mother would say. I began asking parents what they ate at home. Some informed me it depended on how stressed they were when they got home from work-- the extent to which they would cook or not. Others cooked exactly what their children wanted to refrain from arguments. I challenged them. On the days they underwent stress, they were to prepare balanced meals their children already enjoyed. On the days they were

My Child

happy with their accomplishments at work, they were, to introduce new foods. Therefore, their reaction to the new foods would be better received. We know, by our own experiences, on days that are full of chaos and disorder, introducing new concepts can add frustration to a regular routine. And, yet, even others seemed complacent in saying, *"I don't have time to cook,"* or *"I don't know how to cook."* Both these statements were odd to me. My mother worked every day and I don't know where she found time to cook with two children who definitely were quite demanding, but she did. Regardless of what day it was, or what happened, it was routine that while we were occupied with homework, reading, or other things, she was preparing dinner for us. I can't say she was a Michelin star chef. If something was overcooked, she improvised with cutting off the burned parts. If it was dry, we added a little sauce to make it easier to swallow. But, she always made sure we had a balanced meal.

    Kids who eat unbalanced meals suffer all sorts of issues. One alarming issue is the amount of children who are obese. While, a percentage of obesity may be genetic, most cases are preventable. And, again, it goes back to having a healthy balanced lifestyle. We have all sorts of substitutes for nourishment these days, i.e. protein shakes. This leads me to reflect back to my grandmother who grew her own vegetable garden and raised chickens as a source of food. Grocery stores today have an array of food items to choose from, but do we know and understand what's included in the ingredients?

    In addition, to teaching kids about balanced meals being healthy for them, there is also the challenge of convincing them that sleep is essential for optimal development. I remember a student by the name of Jacob. On Mondays, after lunch, he would fall asleep right away. Then, Tuesday through Thursday, he would twist and turn constantly on his cot. I spoke with his father about this, which as it turned out, had difficulty sleeping at home too. I decided to try various methods to get Jacob to understand nap time was important in order to feel energized again. First, I allowed him to work on some computer programs until he became weary -- we tried this for about two weeks, but the results varied. Then, I asked Jacob to tell me what he was thinking about as he was lying down. *"I'm thinking about you...*" he said. Very confused, I asked *"What about me?"* He went on to tell me that I was a robot, and that he and I were going to save the world. At this point, I told him *"You need to give your brain time to recharge, so that we can save the world"*. Unfortunately though, that did not work. Next, I told him to listen to himself breathe and to tell his body and brain he wanted and needed to sleep. It worked somewhat... he would have days that he had shorter naps, but he got rest. Jacob's sleeping pattern continued to mystify me, but I was okay...ole Jacob went on to become one of the highest achievers on the Vanguard test in the history of Erinn's Heart.

As an adult, I know every day will not be the greatest, but as a teacher I must encourage my students to believe it can be. Years have passed and I continue to encourage parents to raise their kids the best way they can. But, I wonder, "Have we given up on our ability to establish a healthy and balanced lifestyle for our children in exchange for convenience?"

CHAPTER FOUR
PLAY

"A child who does not play is not a child, but the man who doesn't play has lost forever the child who lived in him and who he will miss terribly." ~ Pablo Neruda

From the beginning of time playing has always been a favorite pastime. Peter Gray, Boston College developmental psychologist, states that the use of play helped early humans, or "bands" as he called them; to overcome the innate tendencies toward aggression and dominance. *"Play and humor was not just a means of adding fun to their lives. They were means of maintaining the band's existence,"* the band's survival meant skills such as promoting positive attitude, sharing, and peace. The discussion on the forms of play have varied with the evolution of time and man... terms such as free play, structured and unstructured play, learn through play, and the list goes on and on. Free play, Gray states, were those summers and after school hours once relished by the American culture. The children created, chose, and organized their own games without adult intervention not leisure game play such as watching TV, videogames, and extracurricular activities. These free play activities or games in many ways develop a cognitive skill called executive function. This function gives kids the ability to self-regulate.

During my school-age years, I attended St. Therese Catholic School that embraced multi-cultural diversity. The first time I experienced a true melting pot of ethnicities. School was great, the kids were friendly. Everything appeared to be going fine until one day on the playground during recess. My friends and I were playing kickball, our favorite game. The object was to kick the ball as hard as possible. If the ball was caught in the air you were out, if caught rolling three times the same outcome. Now I myself was in a zone…kicking the ball in areas where no one could make a play. The kids were getting upset and figured it was my turn to let someone else kick. But that wasn't how I felt. Then one kid named Stephen ran up to me, calling me offensive names. I don't know if he thought the short kid in glasses and braces was afraid, but surely I wasn't. The next thing I know we were fighting, only moments later to be broken up by the teacher. Both of us were escorted directly to the principal's office. The fact of being in the principal's office didn't really scare me but the idea of my MOTHER being called, sent chills down my spine. Shirley (her name when I was in trouble) walked in calm, listening to every detail the principal and teacher told her. Heart pounding, sweat dripping... I feared the worst. *"She is going to KILL me!"* She politely stood up, told the principal she would be checking me out of school. The entire time walking down the hall, my nerves continued to run amuck.

    We drove home. I know…ALL the way home. Her first words were *"Why are you fighting at school?"* She always wanted to hear my reasoning. There were always three sides to a story--mine, theirs, and the truth; the facts had to be assessed before the punishment. I went on to tell her *"I was fighting because Stephen called me a name"*. She just listened. She stated *"Stephen's words are just words, they can't hurt you… If he didn't touch you, you should not be fighting"*. What she didn't know, is that I experienced embarrassment and was emotionally humiliated. At the age of ten my ability to articulate those feelings was unheard of. Nevertheless, she proceeded with the punishment for the crime--a spanking. Her words of wisdom *"School is a place of learning and not fighting…If you need a reminder I can definitely refresh your memory."*

    After the spanking, tears dried up, we ate lunch and returned to school. *"Now you have a great rest of the day."* Wow, Really? I tell you unconditional love.

    Kids, if they develop great self-regulation skills can control emotions and behavior, resist impulses, exerts self-control and discipline. These findings were based on a study conducted by Elena Bodrova, M.D of Mid-Continent Research for Education and Learning. Researchers have found that play can be creative and liberating, critical and active. But it can also be repetitive, violent, reinforcing status quo or take the form of thinking, wishing or day dreaming. Researchers also suggest only in a specific time, context, a particular performance, play acquires a specific form and function. Internally, the motivated pleasure of playing lies in the playing itself. American children now associate playing as an activity that requires an object. Every child, young and old, loves their toys, which can be a great learning tool. Problem solving, social and verbal are just a few of the skills that can be learned through play. Unfortunately, when kids reach their adolescent years, schools are relied heavily upon to keep students mentally and physically stimulated. Due to budget cuts and poor academic performance, more and more extracurricular activities as well as social clubs are being taken away from schools.

    Children, just as adults, want to be entertained... they want to have fun. Although learning is essential, we must realize that creating a balance is necessary. In the world we live in today, we focus on the content so much that we forget about the entertainment. At times children's interests for activities are lessened due to lack of engaging content. Every parent wants their child to have a fun playful childhood. But, with the competition of today's society to excel, sometimes we see parents living vicariously through their kids. Seeing parents becoming irate at Little League and Pop Warner football games is an example where they believe their kids are having fun, but really are not. We also see extreme parenting on television shows like 20/20, which allows children to pick their own sports or activities while parents are obsessed with their child being superior. Early developmental schools have practiced learning through play in center based form. Center based learning enables children to learn independently through hands on activities in subjects such as math, science, writing, health, art, music and social skills. This concept is beneficial to students in the way of social adaption with their peers and independent problem solving. For many years play was limited to imaginative, creative fun. Now companies realize the impact it can have on children, especially in the areas of gaming and television.

One example, Leap Frog Enterprises is one of the companies that have tapped into this market. In 1995 Michael Wood and Robert Lally founded the company. Woods' son at the age of three had trouble associating letters and their sounds. Woods searched for an educational toy that assisted in his son's development, but did not find anything he thought useful. As a result, he was inspired to develop his own line of educational toys that have continued to evolve with current innovations of the technological age. Television programming such as PBS Kids, Baby TV, and Disney Junior have catered their channels to the fun, educational learning experience that engage children in a variety of learning methods.

For adolescents there is a different approach to play, since they usually have chosen their favorite activities by this time. As with any experience there will be a learning curve in performing at whatever level expected. These experiences build dedication, adaptability, leadership, commitment, and stamina.

Getting involved in your child's play brings more interest to the activity. As parents, we have a tendency to forget our role when playing with our children. Parents are their child's first playmate. Children that play with parents at a young age could possibly continue to involve their parents when they become older. Watching how and what your child is playing with will also help you become aware of their likes and dislikes, which activities they are excelling in or struggling with, and seeing their progress when an activity has an extra level of difficulty. As they master their play we must come up with inventive ways to create a new experience.

However, adolescent play is defined and the rules are already set. The types of play they involve themselves in will have some sort of order. But does it enhance them or influence them negatively? According to Randy Brown, Ph.D., Area Extension Specialist for Children, Youth, and Family Team of University of Nevada, "Extracurricular activities are programs which fulfill two basic conditions:

1. They are not part of the regular school, curricular program;

and
2. They are structured in some way (not just socializing, but working towards some prosocial mission or goal)"

The benefits of your child being involved in extra-curricular activities are tremendous. Some include, getting better grades, attending school regularly, and feeling like they're part of a group. Various experts believe that by staying involved in these enriched programs, teens are less likely to use drugs, dropout of school, and commit crimes. The games, activities, and toys our children enjoy should assist them to grow into adults who understands the rules in the game of life... from the workplace to the sports arena, the need to project good sportsmanship shows they can take defeat or victory with fairness and self-control.

Play is essential. It keeps us growing and engaging with our children as they explore the world around them. Exposing them to new opportunities to play allows us to learn more about our children and assist them in developing healthy competitive traits.

CHAPTER FIVE
LOVE HURTS SOMETIMES

"Love involves a peculiar unfathomable combination of understanding and misunderstanding." ~ Diane Arbus

    Being a parent and giving your child everything you desired growing up can sometimes make or break you. We often remember the "wants" of our childhoods, which at times translates to overcompensation as a parent. Providing excessive "rewards" with no understanding of value or self-initiative may leave an impression of entitlement.

    One particular event stands out in my mind. It was the spring of 1988, stonewashed jeans were in the height of their fashion career. I told my mother that I wanted the famed stone-washed jeans (I know really stone-washed jeans. Don't judge me). Shirley went out, not only purchased one pair, but five. Now I was ecstatic when she walked in the house with them. I could not wait until she handed me that bag. I raced out of the kitchen, into the hallway, bumping into walls, finally slamming the door to my bedroom to try on those jeans. So excited, I opened the door screaming out *"thank you"*. I forgot in all the anticipation, eager to try them on. All of the jeans fit except for the brown pair. I didn't tell my mother those were the pair that I truly wanted. Emerging out of my room a little disappointed, I told her all jeans were fine, except the brown pair. She went on to tell me *"I will return them tomorrow."* I could only hope that she would. The next day came and so did the dreadful news. They were all out of my size. I sulked, pouted, and expressed grimacing faces of disgust. I can only imagine my mother's interpretation of my body gestures, after she went out of her way to not only purchase one pair, but several. Now, imagine the hurt I caused by not being grateful for the pair of jeans that did fit. My sister and I definitely had moments that made my mother feel unappreciated. Regardless how we made her feel, she continued to make us her first priority.

At times parents offer material possessions as their expression of love. But, true love is not solely based on material possessions. It's based on caring, understanding, and committed involvement in developing the true essence of a child while protecting the ones we love. Often, children feel that parents do not love them, because they do not facilitate their every need. But, it's not because they don't want to. There are several reasons why... if everything has already been provided, then what is there to ultimately work for? Some parents praise their child for their accomplishments; some only emphasize the wrong doings. There is easy love, the type of love that a parent can appreciate and enjoy providing. This usually happens when everything seems to be going well. We all love it when our lives are problem free with little stress or tension between parent and child. The other, more common form of love--is known as "tough love", where children at times deviate from the set boundaries and rules that have been established, all the while in need of consistency, coupled with understanding, and firm discipline. As adults, we realize our children can have erratic behavior, *"Yeah, I know."* is one of many answers you'll hear from them in adolescent years. As if they could possibly know everything. This behavior becomes routine unless properly addressed.

Taking a moral stance for what we believe seems to be harder than we think sometimes. Take ABC's show *What Would You Do?* with John Quinones, this show places normal people in morally and ethical compromising situations. Sometimes the responses are jaw-dropping, but real. The hidden camera shows various scenarios from stealing to peer-pressure to discrimination. It's amazing to see how many people reluctantly respond to these situations. "When should we be alarmed by ethical choices?" Ethicist, Lawyer, and Founder of ProEthics, Jack Marshall states,

> "***Ethics Alarms*** are the feelings in your gut, the twinges in your conscience, and the sense of caution in your brain when situations involving choices of right and wrong are beginning to develop, fast approaching, or unavoidable. The better your alarms work and the sooner they start sounding, the more likely you are to do the right thing, or at least to use good ethical reasoning to decide what to do." Parents have gut feelings about their children when irregularities occur in their normal behavior. *"But, do parents seek the reasons behind these irregularities?"* Marshall describes the phrase *everybody does it* as a person's justification for not being accountable for personal ethical judgments. He says, "This rationalization has been used to excuse ethical misconduct since the beginning of civilization. It is based on the flawed assumption that the ethical nature of an act is somehow improved by the number of people who do it, and if "everybody does it," then it is implicitly all right for you to do it as well: cheat on tests, commit adultery, lie under oath, use illegal drugs." Of course, people who use this "reasoning" usually don't believe that what they are doing is wrong because "everybody does it." They usually are arguing that they shouldn't be singled out for condemnation if "everybody else isn't."

As parents, we never want to hear or see our children unhappy or feeling incomplete. But, do we take time to look at what we have given them? Are the tools sufficed to establish a value system? Often children view parents who enforce structure as being "mean." Children should be taught the reality of life where we all have personal joys and struggles. In spite of them, we all can live a life of happiness, regardless of any material possession.

Most loving parents want the best for their child. However, we must consider that exhaustion sets in due to life's demands that interfere with our follow through. We occasionally use the fastest remedy to solve our child problems, "The *Band-Aid* Solution". As Malcolm Gladwell states in *The Tipping Point* "The *Band-Aid* is an inexpensive, convenient, and remarkably versatile solution to an astonishing array of problems. In their history, *Band-Aids* have probably allowed millions of people to keep working or playing tennis or cooking or walking when they would otherwise have had to stop. The Band-Aid solution is actually the best kind of solution because it involves solving a problem with the minimum amount of effort and time and cost."

Sometimes by placing that Band-Aid, we think problems will heal themselves. But, avoiding these situations, just to escape taking on additional stress, may result in long-term complications for you and your child. Children always think they know more than their parents, because they feel that the experiences parents were engaged in are not relevant to current time. And adults don't make this any easier, erasing the memories of their life's lessons instead of using those lessons to help their children gain perspective. Parents need to be all things to their children: a listening ear, a leader, and a friend to help or console them during their time of need. Trust and honesty are the basis of every relationship.

Every interaction is a learning experience. Communication, consistency, and cooperation are three key components to sharing information between humans. Being able to take all information, decipher it to know how to apply it to yourself and your child's life is important. Everybody has their own opinion and views how to raise a child. It should be respected and understood. No one can specify the criteria for a child better than the parent. When families disagree, it places the child in an awkward position of whose advice to take. Mixed messages can be used as a method of manipulation---to get "what they want." In reality, it can tear a family apart. In understanding the distinctive difference between family values and upbringing, adults must communicate their intentions clearly. The purpose for conversing is to present the issues and find solutions. Those solutions should be gathered through unified discussion. As a parent, you give your child choices, but they may not like the results of those choices. One thing is for certain, they've definitely had input.

It was a Thursday morning making my usual visit to the local car wash in Midtown Houston. This particular day was different, Mrs. Charlie, an older lady with the spirit and energy of a twenty-two year old, greeted me. We talked about how our respective businesses were doing, and then she asked if we had ever cared for any adopted children, which seemed odd to me. *"None that I can recall,"* I told her. Only later would I remember we did.

Our conversation began to redirect to her daughter, Nika. Mrs. Charlie gave Nika everything she could within reason, but for some reason Nika always remained defiant. Nika had the curiosity that at times tested her patience. Nika at a very young age had a fiery demeanor. After several of her life's stories, Mrs. Charlie continued to tell me when Nika was fourteen her grandmother had bought her a TV her first one ever. She recalls the event as if it was yesterday, eyes bright, amusement all over her face. *"I heard a loud boom come from Nika's room."* Mrs. Charlie said. Then, Nika came running to tell her *"My TV fell off the dresser by itself!"* Mrs. Charlie asked, *"Is it shattered to pieces?"* Nika told her, *"Yes, it's broken into pieces."* Mrs. Charlie instructed Nika to place the pieces on the street for trash pick-up. And, after disposing of the television, she asked Nika to retrieve a calendar. *"Write this event on your calendar because as long as you live in my house, I will never buy you another TV."* Nika became irate, stating it wasn't her fault. *"Very well then, I just want to prevent another television from falling on its own."* As Nika entered college years later, Mrs. Charlie told her she would buy her a television for her dorm room. Nika was thrilled. Mrs. Charlie bought the television from a local pawn shop. When they arrived, unpacked and set up Nika's room, Nika plugged the television into the outlet. Only to discover it was black and white. Mrs. Charlie just smiled, *"How do you like your new TV?"* Nika had no response. Mrs. Charlie simply smiled and said *"I told you I would buy you a television, but I never promised it would be in color."* When I think about the adopted child for whom we provided service. The child's mother always went above and beyond to please him for his abandonment, but he never even knew the difference.

Sometimes children immediately see inconsistency when families do not work together. When there is not a unified front, the ability to be effective in the delivery of instructions may be misinterpreted. This poses a problem when permission is sought. Families who disagree during their efforts to discipline present more of a problem, than a solution. While youngsters test their parent's limits, they may have difficulty understanding self-control. If parents are too lenient or too strict, kids cannot gauge what the limitations are. Children press the envelope in order to see how much they can get away with. A parent who sets no restrictions will raise a child who continues demanding their wants. "I want a BMW when I reach high school!!" "What am I supposed to buy you for college…A Lamborghini?" What will a child that has everything expect from the world as an adult? On the other side, a parent who is too strict may minimize their child's self-worth. "Whatever I do it's never good enough, I make great grades, I'm respectable… why continue it's never appreciated." Parents need to be clear and fair to themselves as well as the child when ground rules are set.

Children need to see both the nurturing and disciplinary sides of their parents. The nurturer is, of course, preferred by children, because they feel like the nurturer is more understanding to their feelings. While, the disciplinarian is perceived as the "mean one," placing emphasis on the actions that are seen as "wrong". As parents though, if we work at it, we can find a common balance to both.

CHAPTER SIX

IT TAKES A VILLAGE TO RAISE A CHILD

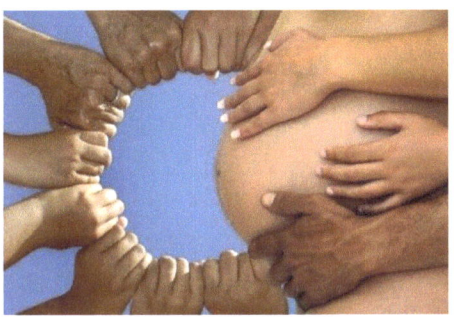

"Every successful individual knows that his or her achievement depends on a community of persons working together."
~ Paul Ryan

During my childhood, I can remember a wide array of people I admired, imitated, and idolized, essentially taking the characteristics of all combined in creating who I wanted to be. Athletes were the Olympians that I read about in Greek Mythology, able to physically rise above unprecedented feats. And as a child, to me Michael Jordan was the pinnacle of godliness. His physical domination over other men who were also professional athletes was like no other in the game of basketball. Jordan even appeared to defy the boundaries of movement in flight. I didn't want to be a basketball player, but it inspired me to be able to defy all laws of reality. His sophomore year his coaches felt he couldn't play at varsity level; instead he was placed onto the junior varsity team. This did not stop Jordan. He used it as motivation to dominate the sport... which he did that year and beyond. He trained ferociously as if never to be denied again. Jordan set a standard of achievement that helped me to develop my own mantra. I stood firm in my belief that no matter what people said, no one could stop me from achieving my goals.

Then there was Michael Jackson; the best entertainer of all time when I was a kid. I would stand in front of the television with a red zipper jacket and a white glove, paying attention to every move he made. Jackson had great stage presence; he connected with his audience in a way many have tried to duplicate, but have failed. His songs were incontestably soul searching. They painted reality through words. And, who can forget his videos that were so captivating. Celebrities often are idolized by children for a number of reasons. Success, wealth, and beauty-- but the list is endless. Even though I admired a lot of them, I related to everyday people; especially those that I interacted with on a consistent basis. It's the values my family instilled in my sister and me that impacted me the most.

My family had the most influential effects upon me. Not because they molded me, but because they never placed judgment. They continued to encourage me, even when problems arose. It may have been easier for them to make the correct decisions for me, but they never would have wanted to belittle me. As an adult, I know my son will imitate, idolize, and admire people. I often ask myself, *"Who will he admire and why?"* and *"Am I presenting an image of self-determination, courage, dedication, strength, and independence that is conscious of others?"* Becoming a source of inspiration and creativity for my son is something I would like to accomplish. I would like for him to be able to look at me and see the attributes he sees in others, i.e. celebrities or other prominent figures. However, when he starts figuring out who he really wants to become, I hope he will reflect upon the examples that I have shown him. As his father, I only want the best for him and for him to understand that I welcome his thoughts, actions, and opinions. For him to know that is something very important to me. At times I know there will be role models that I feel are inappropriate, but I will not chastise him. Right now, he is a young child, but as an adolescent, he will see and hear a wide array of characters. But sometimes in building character, negative images, can help place true role models in a brighter light.

When Erinn and I were growing up, it was unheard of to misbehave in public without someone calling it to the attention of our parents or us -- guidance and teachings of how to be good children wasn't left only to the parent. I recall most adults making sure we were responding and acting appropriately as they thought a child should. I remember my first grade teacher, Sister Donotta, an older woman who was mysteriously stern with us (almost as if my mother talked to her prior about expectations). We knew not to give excuses and accepted being held personally accountable for our actions – knowing very well they could result in us either succeeding or failing. In some ways, it felt like I was her son and she wanted me to outperform everyone. But, did she have those standards for all my classmates? I reflected and can only think she was looking out just for me. However, remember, this sort of expectation seemed to come from every adult I came into contact with. I kept asking myself, *"Did all adults behave like this, or was it the adults that my parents allowed me to be exposed to?"* I always felt as though I was constantly watched or being monitored.

We spent the summers in Vicksburg, Mississippi riding bikes, playing in creeks, and helping my aunt and grandmother in their gardens. Both had the summers off from teaching. My uncle had a farm there too, and I particularly loved working with his pigs and cows. It was a lot of work. We had to feed the animals, clean the pig pens, and cut the grass. My uncle always told us that if we wanted to go to his farm, we had to help, and do the job right. *"Make sure you put the slop in the trough. They have to sleep in the pen!"* I always thought, *"They are pigs. Why do they have to be clean?"* That was just how meticulous he was about his pigs. *"Even though they are pigs, they don't have to live like pigs."* It was so funny to hear him say that when I was younger.

My grandmother bestowed the honor of "Matriarch" from her family; the epitome of goodness. Born in 1911, she had endured a great deal-- always stronger and wiser from the lessons learned. It's no wonder people went to her for guidance and advice. An avid gardener, she possessed the ability to nurture her plants as if they were her own children. Watering them and removing the weeds helped pave the way for their growth. She gardened regularly... no matter the weather. And, that is exactly how she raised her children and grandchildren. She monitored their progress, got to the root of a problem when needed and pulled and discarded the weeds filled with negativity. Just like her garden, if she did not see her children growing in one area, she would try another to see if they would bloom. My Aunt Mary, the psychologist, counselor, and coach -- made sure we got exercise, ate healthy, and behaved. Fighting was not allowed, especially amongst each other. My family believed nothing was so important that family should have to fight. Whatever problems our family had, extended included, were tackled and worked out. My aunt, especially, did not waver in her beliefs. *"Why does my family take every lesson so seriously? Was it that serious?"* I wondered. We all understood the limitations. So, when an opportunity presented itself, we were to take it with gratitude and maximize it. In each of their households we had chores. They were the same in each home and it was expected we do them correctly. Even though some houses had dishwashers, we still had to wash the dishes by hand. We dusted furniture, mopped, and vacuumed the floor. The houses had to be clean, regardless of what time of the day it was. *"We may not have much, but it will be clean,"* That's what my grandmother always said. I remember my mother telling us stories about how the underneath portion of their house had to be just as clean as the inside. Because it sat on bricks, due to flooding, the home was exposed for all to see. Cutting and edging the grass was no easy chore. My aunt and uncle trained us on how this needed to be done. *"If you don't do it right the first time, you will do it again."* They stated. *"The more time you spend doing it wrong, the less time you have to do what you want to do."* This was our lifestyle. The consistent reinforcement played a significant role in our lives.

  It's funny, I recall telling my mother, *"I am going to live in a condo with no grass, and get a maid when I become a grown-up,"* In response she stated, *"It's not that you have to do it when you become a grown up. But, at least, you will know how. You don't know what your financial status will be."* *"I am going to be rich."* I replied. And, she responded *"Even though you may have the money, there is no guarantee it will last."* Yes, my mother was the "Enforcer." All the kids knew she meant business. If for any reason we did not listen and behave, we received punishment from whatever adult was around.

  When Shirley came over on the weekends, you'd better be ready. As the youngest child, she had the stamina of a racehorse and could chase after us if we ran. It was more evident in her stance for my sister and I, just because we were with family or whoever. We behaved the same even in her absence. She knew that family and friends were aiding her as she was single and establishing herself as a professional in the world amidst competition. She did not believe in us being a burden on anyone. People should be excited to see us, not turning their faces regretting when we came around. She drove this rule until we became grown.

As we got older so did our family. And, slowly we started taking over some of the family duties. My uncle, Lee, got really sick and my grandmother started having medical problems, as if starting to wither like her plants. My heart ached and my eyes watered at seeing the pillars of our family start to weaken. It was not how I was accustomed to seeing them. My memories were filled with smiling faces. Now, to see them in pain and weary of making any sort of decision was something new for me. Seldom do you get a chance to see older people interacting and telling stories of their past--giving insight on historical events to children who would otherwise have to read about them in a textbook.

In the world we live in today, we are so afraid to talk about our true feelings, give advice to family and friends about their children, or, even take advice. It seems our world moves so fast nowadays that all we have time for is focusing on our immediate surroundings. But, true, healthy, sustainable relationships between families, schools, and friends are essential for the overall trajectory of your child's growth. We can become overly protective of our children and, although, this is truly understandable -- with so much evil in the world – we have to realize there are good people who want to help our kids too.

Having a good support system is essential. Can you identify yours? Whoever they are, they need to know you'll rely on them to give perspective on our child's problems and interests. Too often we don't ask for help because of our pride, feelings of helplessness, or inadequacy to solve our own children's issues. As parents, we believe we know what they are going through, because they are our own.

However, there is no possible way we can know all of their struggles. Children, like adults, choose to disclose certain information to people they trust. Parents sometimes overlook the value of relationships established by children and their peers. Observing how your children interact with their peers is a good time to gain perspective and insight into your child's world.

We, the parents, are the foundation "the basis on which a child stands or is founded." Support, by definition, is holding in position so as to keep from falling, sinking, or slipping. If not careful though, you can easily cross that line of support--instead, using it as the main source to raise your children. Another area your support system could be beneficial in, is informing you when your emotions are getting the best of you. When do you allow your emotions to take over instead of making rational, thoughtful decisions when the best interest of your child is at stake? Before the people in their support roles can successfully help, we as parents have to make a true commitment to listen to their advice.

In a society where there are so many problems-- from obesity to bullying to suicide and mental illness to physical challenges; parents first have to be conscious of the signs their children may be giving out as a cry for help or attention. Like anyone who has our best interest at heart, our support systems will only be willing to be as committed, as we are. People will always extend more help, if they see the dedication of parents and effort from the children. Keeping your emotions in check will show your kids how to manage their emotions. This can be difficult, but it is extremely vital. Ask yourself, how do you build self-awareness, self-discipline and self-motivation? Teachers deal with these questions everyday like us parents. From an educator's point of view, when speaking with my son's teacher, I realized his behavior was one way with me and different with others.

When dealing with the parents of my students, the advice I usually gave dealt with the limitations and boundaries I set in the classroom, and the rest of the school. I wanted parents to understand the goals I set forth were attainable and that I only expected their child's best efforts. A child recognizes leadership in an adult that displays it. Every child responds differently, but the important characteristic is consistency.

Every child has a distinctive personality, and no one should try to take their individual identity away. Only when there is potential for harm, intervention may be needed. *How does your child's behavior differ from you, compared to others? Why?* By addressing any issues early on, children will have the basis with which to rationalize and make suitable decisions. There will be times when things happen in their life and the people you leave in charge of your child will have to make key decisions. If children see and understand that all the adults in their life have the same approach and beliefs as you, then they'll receive the constant reinforcement needed to help them make more right than wrong choices. For instance, while growing up, I remember all of my mother's support team having input on my sister and I. My mother worked countless hours with her job, so she had to rely on her support team to reinforce her methods. Family members, friends, and teachers all made my mom aware of our progress or regress. As far back as I can remember those were the people that impacted my life.

On the weekends we traveled to Vicksburg, Mississippi where my extended family lived. It was country living at its best. Life in Vicksburg was simple and there were not many distractions. My grandmother worked as a cook for a nearby head start program. My Uncle Lee worked at a lumber mill down the street from where he and his family lived. My Aunt Mary worked at another neighboring head start. While my Uncle John, a military man, worked as a coach and teacher across the state line in Louisiana. My Aunt Hazel was an accountant who worked in Jackson. Almost every weekend the entire family was together. From all of them, we learned about work ethic and the true meaning of hard work. Looking back I understand it helped me become confident and self-sufficient. They seldom journeyed into town, unless it was mandatory as they truly lived from the land. I remember all of my aunts, uncles, and grandmother receiving weekly highlights, and lowlights, on how my sister and I were performing. Each responded by congratulating the accomplishments and encouraging discussions on problems that needed sorting through. They made us aware of the opportunities that we had. When they gave us a history lesson, it wasn't a story we heard in textbooks. It was their real life stories. They always stressed the importance of education, which today people seem to take for granted. They faced various challenges -- just getting to and from school were difficult, along with the strain of making friends from other racial backgrounds. The consequences of having friends of other races were detrimental for them. They faced violence for being in favor of racial equality, and when they applied themselves in the classroom, they were often ridiculed -- just because they wanted to better themselves academically. When we heard these stories we thought them to be extreme, but these were common day-to-day problems for them. As a young child, their stories didn't really register. But, as an adult, I wonder, *"If I was stripped of all my belongings, would I have the will and tools to survive in this world?"* Survival to them meant something entirely different from what I believe survival to be. Making sure their family was safe, had food to eat, clean clothes to wear and a roof over their heads – that's what survival meant to them. None of these things had to be top of the line or name brand. They just needed to be reliable.

  As children, my sister and I wanted numerous items that we thought to be popular and my mother always tried her best to attain them. My family spoiled us, but they believed in spoiling as a form of reward if we truly earned it. Today, we reward our children just for showing up to school, sporting events, or even simply participating. This was never the case for me while growing up. If we participated, then it was expected we gave our very best. However, if we failed, their words consoled the hurt we were feeling. They didn't believe in quitting. If we didn't succeed at something, we figured out why together, so that the next time we experienced progress. They were always in our corner as long as we gave our all. Our village was primarily our family. The support, lessons, and insight we received from them has built our infrastructure as people.

We are worldlier because of their need to educate and engage us in the reality of life. Your village may be smaller or larger, but the most important thing to remember that YOU create the village. The village that you create must align your rules and expectations with consistent reinforcement and rewards. Your village is only as effective as you require it to be.

CHAPTER SEVEN
MORE UNITES US THAN DIVIDES US

"Unity is strength... when there is teamwork and collaboration, wonderful things can be achieved." ~ Mattie Stepanek

Fast forward to the year 2012. We continue to subcategorize children with the intent for them to have self-identification. In continuing to practice this way of thinking, we have allowed public perception of stereotypes to influence their minds. For centuries we have based this upon limited information. Why do people stereotype? Stereotypes can be detrimental. Every day, children in America are labeled and categorized based on status. Unfair it seems, since no one group has a less or greater chance of success. Stereotypes are simply an opening of the door for prejudices against, or for a particular group. Is this a fair assessment before children have the chance to establish themselves? With every new source of information people misuse and misinterpret, children are unfairly judged. Children are born into different conditions of which they have no control. They are taught the family's values and are expected to live up to the standards of the environment. All children come into this world unbiased and untainted, the difference is the parent's environment and access to useful information. There were countless struggles in the past where people were denied their rights' to have or gain access to information to better themselves and their children. Ethnic groups throughout

history have been faced with severe adversity, some even resulting in death.
 Let's take a quick trip down history lane. The history of the United States starts with the thirteen colonies declaring their freedom from British rule in 1776 through the Declaration of Independence. Now the thirteen colonies were made up whites who fought against other whites, the difference--one was American, the other was British. The Thirteen colonies won the American Revolutionary War as a result of wanting their freedom. African-American history began with African slaves brought to Virginia to serve as domestics in the 1600s. For years slaves were freed, while some fled. Even though African-Americans were freed according to the Emancipation Proclamation, still they were tortured, not given equal rights until the civil rights movement decades later. Latinos and Hispanics existence in America dates back to the second longest presence in the United States. The Spaniards occupied most of the southern region of the United States in the first conquest of the nation. During the Mexican-American war and American Revolution they lost lands to the United States. Asian-Americans arrived during the gold rush and railroad expansion in 1850's and 1860's. They received attacks from Irish Americans who were immigrants as well. The Asian-Americans fled to sanctuary in large cities they called Chinatowns, small communities where they received less hostility. The Native American, the first occupants whose numbers begin to decline at the arrival of the European explorers and colonists who brought disease, warfare, and ultimately committing genocide. Internal conflicts within tribes caused its people to experience near extinction. So as we see, we all have a common history, in that we all struggled, fought, and died to establish ourselves. It is a basic trait embedded in the behavior of evolution--survival of the fittest "only the strong survive". So why do we continue to have internal conflict within one nation "Our America".
 Questions of children receiving equal opportunities still raise alarm. *Are "ALL" children receiving a fair chance at the American Dream?* People would say "yes". The reality is the culture of limited thinking in the face of facts has not been changed. Each race is

depicted with positive and negative images in media, literature, theater, and other creative expressions. These depictions present real repercussions for each group during daily interactions with the "real-world". Some of the images that are portrayed do not show the accurate reports of each race.

Media is generated to give mass people information of the events happening directly and indirectly in their lives. Beginning when our children are in their critical learning stages, they're starting to soak up information being broadcasted to them. The media shows and tell stories from various angles... giving what they feel is complete up-to-the-minute information. Cartoons, reality TV, and other programming – while they can be entertaining -- can fill a child's head with fantasy and violence. The reality is that unless there is adult supervision to explain "right" from "wrong," children view what their watching as a form of truth. Kids do not immediately have the ability to decipher key pieces of information like adults. And sometimes even as adults, we do not gather the necessary research to find out the truth behind any particular story.

How does the media keep stereotypical culture alive? Television has programming that shows different sources of empowerment and negative interpretation of culture. The young are portrayed more often in a negative image, than a positive one.

EthnicMajority.com, a minority empowerment organization, states:

> "Who we see, hear, and read on television, radio, newspapers, and in movies has a great deal of influence on shaping the attitudes of all Americans. How African, Hispanic (Latino), and Asian Americans are portrayed in these mediums often stereotypes and reinforces negative images of each ethnic group."

The main reason every generation feels that the next one is lost, is that, as adults, we only see the shortcomings through what the media shows and tells us. Children view television, magazines, and videos hoping to make a connection with someone that's like them economically, racially, and culturally. Sometimes, they have difficulty relating to other kids different from them, because of the stereotypes they see in mainstream media. They may view other cultures, unworthy of exploration, because of perceptions and beliefs presented to them; without even attempting to seek the truth on their own. Overall, children are doing a great job of being assimilated, in spite of how they may see their culture portrayed on television.

America being a capitalist nation, media understands the bottom line equates to dollars and cents. Business is business. Some experts though believe they are doing it at the expense of showing certain groups at a disadvantage by portraying them negatively. Media equals social approval for kids. If they see people on TV doing something, then it must be ok. Only thing though, as adults, we know this to be false. Networks air what they believe people want to see – the more popular the show, the more money they make off advertisements. While advertisers are seeking to target specific demographics who watch these shows, children can only interpret the messages from a limited perspective. Children need the regulation of parents to talk to them about what they see, hear, and the message it relays. Television can influence us on things we eat to what we do in our free time. While writing this book, I actually felt that the next generation was lost as well. But, I was only thinking about the images shown by the media not reflecting on my own childhood.

On television, minorities were often depicted as growing up in low-income households with inadequate food sources. Media can be biased on the information it broadcasts. Putting our kids on a media diet can help reduce any misinterpretations of cultures. Not all whites have access to the best jobs and schools. Not all blacks are walking around selling drugs and playing sports, hoping to make it to the pros. Not all Asians are gifted with the knack for medicine or engineering. And, not all Hispanics grow up to cut grass. Native Americans are not all alcoholics living on reservations with casinos. It's natural for children to mimic things they see others doing. If all they see are ways of living introduced to them via television and other forms of media, then they will mimic them.

Monitoring your child's consumption of media is vital, especially while they're still forming their own ideas, opinions, and understanding of the world around them. Explaining what they sometimes hear on television or read in publications may not necessarily be real. Most stories shown may be extreme cases of good or bad. The goals of media range from trying to sell items to informing and entertaining you and your child and the list continues to grow. Parents need to understand they hold the key to their child's success -- and how much exposure and access to television shows, radio programming, or the internet they have. Most homes in the U.S. have some form of media. Children will want access to use them, but the key factor is you and boundaries you set. Alternatives to these forms of media that stimulate the mind and body extend from physical activity to reading to communicating with other positive peers. Numerous efforts have been put in place to reduce stereotypical threats. Especially in the classroom, where we hear how children are constantly underperforming, the Regional Educational Laboratory in Greensboro, North Carolina has found statistically positive effects of intervention by using intervention strategies such as:

- Reinforcing students the idea that intelligence is expandable and, like a muscle, grows stronger when worked.
- Teach students that their difficulties in school are often part of a normal "learning curve" or adjustment process, rather than something unique to them or their racial group.
- Help students reflect on other values in their lives beyond school that are sources of self-worth for them.

Question: How are American students performing in reading?

Average reading scale score of 4th-, 8th-, and 12th-graders, by sex and race/ethnicity: Selected years, 1992 through 2009

Selected student characteristic	1992[1]	1994[1]	1998	2000	2002	2003	2005	2007	2009	+/- Variance
4th-graders, all students										
Total	217	214	215	213	219	218	219	221	221	+4
Race/ethnicity										
White	224	224	225	224	229	229	229	231	230	+6
Black	192	185	193	190	199	198	200	203	205	+13
Hispanic	197	188	193	190	201	200	203	205	205	+8
Asian/Pacific Islander	216	220	215	225	224	226	229	232	235	+19
American Indian/Alaska Native	‡	211	‡	214	207	202	204	203	204	-7
8th-graders, all students										
Total	260	260	263	—	264	263	262	263	264	+4
Race/ethnicity										
White	267	267	270	—	272	272	271	272	273	+6
Black	237	236	244	—	245	244	243	245	246	+9
Hispanic	241	243	243	—	247	245	246	247	249	+8
Asian/Pacific Islander	268	265	264	—	267	270	271	271	274	+6
American Indian/Alaska Native	‡	248	‡	—	250	246	249	247	251	+3
12th-graders, all students										
Total	292	287	290	—	287	—	286	—	288	-4
Race/ethnicity										
White	297	293	297	—	292	—	293	—	296	-1
Black	273	265	269	—	267	—	267	—	269	-4
Hispanic	279	270	275	—	273	—	272	—	274	-5
Asian/Pacific Islander	290	278	287	—	286	—	287	—	298	+8
American Indian/Alaska Native	‡	274	‡	—	‡	—	279	—	283	+9

— Not available.
‡ Reporting standards not met. [1] Accommodations were not permitted for this assessment.
Amended Table: Gender removed from table. Variance Added by Author.
[1]Testing accommodations (e.g., extended time, small group testing) for children with disabilities and English language learners were not permitted during this assessment.

Question: How are American students performing in science?

Average science scale scores and percentage of 4th-, 8th-, and 12th-graders 2005 attaining science achievement levels, by selected student characteristics: 1996, 2000, and 2005

Selected characteristic	4th-graders			
	1996[1]	2000	2005	+/- Variance
Total	147	147	151	+4
Race/ethnicity				
White	158	159	162	+4
Black	120	122	129	+9
Hispanic	124	122	133	+9
Asian/Pacific Islander	144	‡	158	+14
American Indian	129	135	138	+9

Selected characteristic	8th-graders			
	1996[1]	2000	2005	+/- Variance
Total	149	149	149	+0
Race/ethnicity				
White	159	161	160	+1
Black	121	121	124	+3
Hispanic	128	127	129	+1
Asian/Pacific Islander	151	153	156	+5
American Indian	148	147	128	-20

Selected characteristic	12th-graders			
	1996[1]	2000	2005	+/- Variance
Total	150	146	147	-3
Race/ethnicity				
White	159	153	156	-3
Black	123	122	120	-3
Hispanic	131	128	128	-3
Asian/Pacific Islander	147	149	153	+6
American Indian	144	151	139	-5

‡ Reporting standards not met.

[1] Testing accommodations (e.g., extended time, small group testing) for children with disabilities and limited-English-proficient students were not permitted on the 1996 science assessment. Amended Table: Gender removed from table. Variance Added by Author.

SOURCE: U.S. Department of Education, National Center for Education Statistics. (2011). *The Digest of Education Statistics, 2010* (NCES 2011–015), Table 148.

Question: How are American students performing in math?

National Center for Education Statistics
Table A-24-2. Average mathematics scale scores, by grade and selected student and school characteristics: Selected years, 1990–2011

Student or school characteristic	Grade 4			+/- Variance
	1990[1]	2009	2011	
Race/ethnicity				
White	220	248	249	+29
Black	188	222	224	+36
Hispanic	200	227	229	+29
Asian/Pacific Islander	225	255	256	+31
Asian	‡	‡	257	-
Native Hawaiian/Pacific Islander	‡	‡	236	-
American Indian/Alaska Native	‡	225	225	0

Student or school characteristic	Grade 8			+/- Variance
	1990[1]	2009	2011	
Race/ethnicity				
White	270	293	293	+23
Black	237	261	262	+25
Hispanic	246	266	270	+24
Asian/Pacific Islander	275	301	303	+28
Asian	‡	‡	305	-
Native Hawaiian/Pacific Islander	‡	‡	269	-
American Indian/Alaska Native	‡	266	265	-1

Student or school characteristic	Grade 12			+/- Variance
	2005	2009	2011	
Race/ethnicity				
White	157	161	—	+4
Black	127	131	—	+4
Hispanic	133	138	—	+5
Asian/Pacific Islander	163	175	—	+12
Asian	—	—	—	—
Native Hawaiian/Pacific Islander	—	—	—	—
American Indian/Alaska Native	134	144	—	+10

— Not available.
‡ Reporting standards not met. [1] Accommodations were not permitted for this assessment.
Amended Table: Gender removed from table. Variance Added by Author.

[1]Testing accommodations (e.g., extended time, small group testing) for children with disabilities and English language learners were not permitted during this assessment

NOTE: Average mathematics scale scores include public and private school students. At grades 4 and 8, the National Assessment of Educational Progress (NAEP) mathematics scale ranges from 0 to 500. The framework for the 12th-grade mathematics assessment was revised in 2005; as a result, the 2005 and 2009 results cannot be compared with those from previous years. The 12th-grade mathematics assessment was not administered in 2011. At grade 12, mathematics scores on the revised assessment range from 0 to 300. For more information on NAEP, see Appendix B – *Guide to Sources*. Race categories exclude persons of Hispanic ethnicity. For more information on race/ethnicity or free or reduced-priced lunch, see Appendix C – *Commonly Used Measures*.

According to the report *American Students Show Steady Progress in Math, Rank High in International Education Comparison TIMSS* "American students in grades four and eight showed steady improvements in mathematics since 1995 and generally rank at least in the top one-third compared to other countries, according to an international education comparison released today. In the latest report of the Trends in International Mathematics and Science Study (TIMSS), the ongoing evaluation of 36 to 48 countries revealed that in 2007 the U.S. consistently rated at least in the top one-third and in some cases the top one-fourth of participating nations. In 2007, the average U.S. fourth-grade math score was higher than those of students in 23 of 35 other countries and among eighth-graders was higher than students in 37 of 47 other countries." "Today's TIMSS results reconfirm what we have long known—if we set high expectations, our children will rise to the challenge," said U.S. Secretary of Education Margaret Spellings. "I am encouraged that U.S. students are improving, and particularly that many children who were once left behind are now making some of the greatest gains in math."

All of these predetermined assumptions of people are misleading portrayals to our youth. As we can see from the facts and data all of American children are progressing. Children don't enter this world programmed to feel superior or less significant than the other. They only know what they see during parental interactions and the exposure from the outside world. Even with the vast knowledge from scientific research to discredit these teachings, we continue the cycle. Leaders and activists work vigorously to inform all of America of the contributions from all Americans, not one specific ethnicity. For fear of the unknown, we tend to allow these methods to remain active. As history has shown us each race has had its own personal struggle with other races to establish their place in America. We continue to fight amongst each other, even though we all strive for better lives. Our extension to the people, who want help and change, will continue to contribute to the betterment of all mankind. We are in a place in time where policies attempt to protect us from any form of discrimination. Nonetheless, we still alienate the less efficient people as non-productive and worthless, without cultural considerations. We must provide tangible resources to help empower people in these communities. Exposure to diverse cultures provides children the opportunity to learn and appreciate different cultures, traditions, and languages. This exposure ultimately helps to break down barriers of misperception presented by misleading stereotypes that have been viewed and distorted for centuries. Cultural reassurance in diverse settings offers the ability to adapt and understand the actions of individuals. Insecurities are feelings we all face at some point, but reducing anxiety outside of the comfort of our environment has to be addressed. In order for everyone to advance, cultures must be shared. Trends occur in specific situations, however true information is gathered by the people living within the culture--not the individuals observing it. Fabrication of the truth restricts a clear evaluation of a culture. Empathy towards human life should not only be addressed as an emotion, but an opportunity to inspire. Everyone has misfortunes in life that allows people to construct character. A life of happiness is obtained by sharing and learning differences to formulate personal understandings. When we change our thought process, we change our beliefs of what seems to be true. Once our beliefs have been altered we have new expectations. New expectations bring a brighter attitude towards people. A brighter attitude brings a revised behavior. Revised behavior optimizes performance. Optimized performance brings new life for our children's future; no matter their background, social class, or environment.

CHAPTER EIGHT
ORGANIZATIONAL LEARNING

"It is good to rub and polish our brain against that of others"
~ Michel de Montaigne

A learning organization is one in which people are continuously learning and transforming. It has a heightened capability to learn, adapt, and change. Learning processes are analyzed, developed, monitored, and aligned with the innovative goals of the organization. Most companies use this type of business model, because it has been proven to be successful. So, why can't families along with educators use this concept to increase the overall understanding of children's development?

A report from the National Center for Education Statistics reveals, "Many Americans believe that urban schools are failing to educate the students they serve. Even among people who think that schools are doing a good job overall are those who believe that in certain schools, conditions are abysmal. Their perception, fed by numerous reports and observations, is that urban students achieve less in school, attain less education, and encounter less success in the labor market later in life."

Why are conditions terrible? We live America, where funding "we would think" could provide every child equal access to healthy learning environments. Why are urban kids viewed as achieving less and encountering less success career-wise? What is the rural and suburban vantage point? If they are performing better, why are they not sharing information? Is it not true that districts, states, the nation receive money from the same source? Or...Is it allocated more in specific areas? Why can't concepts and practices be shared to optimize each school within a district? Why can't the same accountability be set for all schools? The phrase organizational learning has been tossed around from government to private companies to schools. The concept is an ideal that every person involved will prosper... each employee strengthening the link to the chain of success.

Most Americans share a common goal for their children: to make sure they're safe, in good health, have food and shelter. In America, the land of the plentiful, homelessness still exists, and families' are suffering from hunger or may not have access to healthcare. Experts believe poverty equates to obesity, poor education, and crime. According to www.forbes.com, "Mississippi is the poorest state based on per capita income." And, furthermore, the Robert Wood Johnson Foundation states, "Investing in prevention today will mean a healthier tomorrow for our children."

As of 2012, Mississippi leads the nation in obesity rates, reliance of food stamps, and low academic standings. Whereas, New Hampshire is on the completely opposite end of the spectrum. "Why such disproportion?"...I wonder. Brainstorming continues to be the centerpiece of problem solving. The exchange of information between several minds creates new ideas and develops applicable concepts. By simply placing these minds together doesn't guarantee efficiency, unless a common goal is pre-determined. Sharing the best, worst, and random ideas...... (Thinking outside the box), uncovers potential solutions, problems, and releases fresh ideas. This free flow of ideas begins transformation......"How do we get people motivated to change..... to better themselves?" America can provide the resources. But, it's up to us to take advantage of them. This leads me back to organizational learning in which commitment is needed from the people within an organization in order to empower change. Change is difficult for anyone, especially for children. But, showing them how to embrace change can open new doors to opportunity.

John Maxwell presents an equation E+R=O (events plus response equals outcome). Some of the events we encounter are unpreventable, leaving us with a bitter taste of reality. But, we have the choice to respond in multiple ways, giving us varied outcomes. For example, let's say my son's preschool suddenly shut down. This school was not the most convenient, but because of its excellent academic and kid-friendly social development programs, diversity and price; we made it our primary choice. But after the event, we now had to respond. Should we, A.) Choose to send him to a school closest to our home for convenience, even though it compromises his education? B.) Pay for him to go to private school in the same area where his former preschool was located? or C.) Drive 10-15 minutes longer to a school that has the identical characteristics of the one that shut down? Tina and I weighed the three options and ultimately decided on "C". It presented the balance we needed. Being part of an organization does not mean you are subject to stay in that environment if the organization is not helping you to meet the goals for your child.

Carol Dweck of Stanford University keyed a term "Fixed Mindset vs. Growth Mindset". Fixed Mindset "they are the way they are" where intelligence is stagnant. It is not that children don't want to aspire for the same goals and accomplishment of others but they feel and think because of who they are, they are limited. So they only seek out the challenges where low risk is involved. Growth Mindset whereas intelligence is ever developing through adaptive experiences brought on by setbacks, obstacles, and failures. These people have the innate skill to learn and improve. We praise our children for their "smart" ability thinking this positive reinforcement has a positive outcome of performance. When encouraging our children we understand that not every task they will perform exceptional at, but giving their best effort to make the best outcome of the situations. We must continue to be facilitators of growth mindset promotion in order for our children to gather techniques to flourish.

In some instances visions are ahead of their time. Throughout the years from government to innovators, all have attempted to close the gap for all American children from Goals 2000: Educate America

Act signed by President Clinton to No Child Left Behind Act signed by President George W. Bush. Our government has consciously done everything within their power to create innovative ways to bridge gaps. Each wave of reorganizing of policies to fix the problem of equality in classrooms throughout America has still been elusive to the most brilliant minds that lead this great nation. As a new wave of innovators such as Salman Khan who founded *Khan Academy*, offers a "free world-world class education for anyone anywhere" online. Others like Will Allen founder of *Growing Power*, "a national non-profit organization and land trust supporting people from diverse backgrounds, and the environments in which they live, helping to provide equal access to healthy, high quality, safe and affordable food for people in all communities". These are two of the many visionaries, through their ingenious techniques have redefined our outlook on how ordinary people can impact the world through sheer determination of wanting equal access to everyone.

Change comes from two places: either inspiration or out of desperation. As parents, we strive to inspire our children to seize the best out of life. At times we act out of desperation attempting to reach those goals. Desperation usually lasts through the time of turmoil, then once out of the storm everything goes back to some sort of normalcy. Inspiration is driven by motivation, imbedded internally, and gives that drive you need to strive for better results in whatever you do. Ultimately, children see the greatness in what the world has to offer and are passionate about what their life can become. Children are conceived expectantly and unexpectedly, but regardless, each child can believe in, experience, and activate greatness.

Poor, middle, and upper class parents all face the same pressure. All want to provide the best opportunities for their kids. The drive to overcome social pressures cannot be taught. It's an inner strength that's acquired through experiences. The question though is, "How can we expect children to be open to change and persevere when the adults in their lives refuse to do so?" The only way to change cultural mentality is for individuals to learn and participate. Programs are established with the intention to empower people. So, why is Mississippi's system failing, while New Hampshire's system is flourishing? To make sure programs are using the best techniques possible for our kids--and being held accountable if they do not, parents really need to get involved. The reality is that all states should be equally excelling to keep the United States competitive in the global scheme of things. As an educator, I truly understand the impact and responsibility of providing a model structure that allows teachers, staff, and students to reach the next level.

CHAPTER NINE
IF AT FIRST YOU DON'T SUCCEED, TRY, TRY, AGAIN

"Failure means a stripping away of the inessential"
~ J.K. Rowling

Failure can be a confusing concept. Although unwanted; there can be no success without it. For most, failure is not thought of as a step along the way to success, but as a barrier to future pursuits. Instead of feelings of inadequacy, one can focus on making the necessary changes to improve future outcomes. Turning our dreams into reality may seem far-fetched at times, because life can be unfair. So we place our dreams on hold in hopes of the perfect scenario. NEWS FLASH! There are no "perfect scenarios", only opportunities people take by the horns and try, try again, until they find a way to make them work. Adults are quick to instruct children to work hard and give their best effort. But as adults, sometimes things we attempt do not always produce the desired results; leaving us to think, *"All that work I put in and I failed?"*; only to see someone else with the same concept or idea become a success. In comparing ourselves constantly with others, we figure that we are entitled to the same successes. In most cases we are not aware of the intangibles that help to make that small distinctive difference.

Children, like adults experience humiliation when they are unsuccessful in attempting new tasks. But are they constructing a template based on what they figure to be correct? Or are they constantly making revisions based on the results from failed attempts?

My Child

Success stories usually highlight the achievements that result in success. People usually don't want to hear about setbacks before reaching those achievements. Truth be told, shame and humiliation are emotions associated with failure. And sometimes these emotions make us feel worthless and unproductive, which can be viewed by many as being a dreamer and never able to accomplish anything. But without dreamers --- those who think outside of the box and willing to take risks; innovation is not possible. Innovation is spurred by these same dreamers and believers of change. Adults can help children accept setbacks and to improve on the lessons learned. Our children must understand that gaining comprehensive, efficient, and accurate information is the first step to reducing the probability of failure.

Children tend to make things harder than they are. If the techniques seem to be more complex than normal, then we as parents should assist. In order for them to feel confident, attainable steps and goals should be met first. This will cut down on the overwhelming aspect of the big picture, instead allowing them to concentrate on working step by step until their project is completed. Organization is critical. This creates a strategic game plan. Useless interruptions from others can easily disrupt the learning process. So, having teachers that can manage learning environments is important. Do you remember the jokesters of the class? I do. And, which teacher tolerated them and the ones who didn't? For me it was Sister Donotta--she was no nonsense.

Success means different things to different people. We are a society that specializes in everything. Do not make the mistake of burdening your child with your delayed accomplishments. He/she will already feel full of anxiety. Talk to them about figuring out the source of their problems. As I write this chapter I think of a friend Jason. Michael, Jason's son, from a previous marriage lived with his mom until the age of fourteen. He began having trouble focusing in school and home. His mother reached out to Jason in an attempt to help Michael regroup. Jason welcomed Michael with open arms and iron fist. He told Michael he would not tolerate the behavior he exhibited while living with his mom. Life became good for the both of them; Jason had his oldest son with whom he could help mold. Michael had the strength of the father; he needed to help him refocus. School became interesting as well as athletics. Michael started to find his way, until the demons of Jason's alcohol problems re-emerged. They began to argue over every minor or major detail, things were getting really bad. Michael's old habits too began to make themselves present. Jason continued to chastise his son for his faults, while he was facing his own. He sent Michael back to his mother, and instead of facing his own problems. In my opinion, I felt Jason gave up on himself and his son. Jason's decision to plant the seeds of his expectation was essential to Michael's progress. But, his inability to monitor his own behavior, allowed the unwanted weeds to take over their garden. Michael had just begun to dream of a new life, only to be taken away. What will his other children think? What will become of their dreams?

While growing up, I knew that I wasn't great at everything, but I gave my all. Most times I only performed average... at best. I wasn't a star athlete or an academic scholar or even the social elite. I was an ordinary boy with dreams of being somebody that made a difference. Despite not being the best athlete in school or the valedictorian, exposure was never the reason for me not to excel. From elementary to high school I was actively involved in sports, academics and social activities, but my mother didn't really stress one over the other. As long as my grades were good, she was happy. As a child I always wanted to be great at everything, but was that even possible? I looked at my friends who played sports and I tried my best to be as awesome, but it never quite worked out that way. The same was the case with my classes and social outings. I looked at sports as something fun. I didn't have the overpowering pressure from my family to be the best football player in order to receive a scholarship...and my mom didn't feel the need for me to be at every social gathering in order to be the most popular. What she did emphasize was "effort!" And, if they did not meet her expectations, then she sought help so that I could become a better individual. Even if she was unaware of the balance she was providing in my life, she did it. And at one point, my motto became, "I don't want to be great at one thing, but really good at everything." This helped me focus on the things I was good at, which truly limited my chances of failure.

"When do you take the signs children give and act accordingly to the situation?" "When do you separate yourself from distractions? And limit the noise to have the ability to process that information." As parents we have to regain control over distractions. In order to prevent potential harm to our children, as many of us do in our respective fields.

As a Chief Financial Officer, I don't wait until the end of the year to process and deliver methods of clearing discrepancies in budget accountability. A doctor would not diagnose a patient with pancreatic cancer without conducting the appropriate tests. As professionals we continue to make ourselves aware of the signs and symptoms.

My Uncle Lee was a strong man... who never believed his body would weaken. So when I heard of his illness from smoking and exposure to asbestos, I was afraid. According to the doctor, the smoking along with the asbestos had been affecting him for years. When he was finally diagnosed, he was in the advanced stages of pancreatic cancer. He had insurance, so why did he ignore the signs? The stomach pain and weight loss, but it was too late.......JUANDICE!!!! Eventually he was admitted into Baptist Medical Center where he continued to suffer. My family and I traveled to Jackson to see him. As he laid there on his bed, we could only pray for the miracle of medicine to help his ailing body. "Uncle Lee, don't worry everything will be fine." I told him. Hoping the words would bring him comfort. I loved him. He was the strongest man I knew. He was 64 years old when he passed away. My uncle's fear of consulting a doctor, because of the possibility of hearing unsettling news was an eye opener to our family. Where was my Uncle Lee that feared no challenge; the man that frowned in the face of failure?

Children receive information in the same way as adults. Helping them to process cause and effect will prevent them from "running into the brick wall" over and over again. The same actions usually give the same results. I recall a pair of three-year-old twins whose parents were highly educated and attentive to their children. One day they arrived at school, Chelsea, one of the girls, said the words "Fuck this." Another little girl, Denise, repeated it, and immediately the other children responded by telling Mrs. Nguyen. Who addressed the children by simply stating "Those are not words we use. You are never to repeat those words anywhere." She did not place emphasis on the inappropriateness of the words. Several hours later on the playground the same words were used by her twin sister, Sophia. This time, I was informed from the students, so I made Sophia aware of the same inappropriate use of language and placed her in time out. Giving her time to reflect on her verbal language and think about the consequences. That afternoon I spoke with their mother about the new vocabulary words they learned. She was confused where they were picking up these types of words, because they were constantly monitoring their surroundings, or so they thought. She eventually found out where the twins had learned the words at "her local gym". She informed me she would no longer be taking the children to that location. I went on to tell her "By taking your children out doesn't solve the problem, make the staff aware that you heard your children say these words. And keep an ear out". She took my advice not only fixing her personal dilemma with her children, but provided alertness to the staff.

      As we attempt to meet the needs of each child, sometimes we are limited to understanding other varied contributions. Why do some children learn and others do not? Who are the gifted, average and the least academically poised students? Are students being challenged based on personal needs? According to the study, "Praise for Intelligence Can Undermine Children's Motivation and Performance", Claudia M. Mueller and Carol S. Dweck state, "Praise for ability is commonly considered to have beneficial effects on motivation. Contrary to this popular belief, six studies demonstrated that praise for intelligence had more negative consequences for students' achievement motivation than praise for effort."

Are children only seeking out the challenges where low risk is involved? Is self-esteem compromised if they think they will fail? Criticism is often viewed as a reflection of who they are. Effort is demoralizing if no progress has been achieved. Individuals learn through experiences. We are reluctant to take on changes due to fear of the unknown or fear of failure. As parents, are we promoting the fear of failure? Or are we promoting "only try if I know I will succeed". Intelligence is acquired through experiences and exposure. Failures and Successes will happen... As a result we must prepare our children.

CHAPTER TEN
THE WONDER YEARS

"My teenage years were exactly what they were supposed to be. Everybody has their own path. It's laid out for you. It's just up to you to walk it." ~ Justin Timberlake

As children develop, communication becomes more important than ever. During this developmental time, parents should be prepared to talk to their children honestly and candidly about changes, especially their bodies. And, it's more important to hear this information from their parents as opposed to hearing untrue statements from their friends.

According to www.livestrong.com, "Puberty is a time in a young person's life when hormones are on the increase leading to physical and emotional changes." Boys will grow hair throughout their body, experience erections, and vocal changes. Girls will begin to grow breasts and have their periods. Both sexes will experience natural sexual urges... this being the tip of the iceberg.

Equally important is talking to your children about addictions, temptations, and making the right choices. When your child starts experiencing pleasures – whether food, drugs, or sex – their brain remembers this and wants to repeatedly feel the same sensations. This, of course, can lead to addiction if children do not learn to identify their temptations and how to control their desires.

"An individual faces a self-control dilemma whenever the attainment of an alluring desire or temptation would conflict with more important, longer goals (Ainslie, 1992; Loewnstein, 1996; Rachlin, 2000; Thaler, 1991; Trope & Fishbach, 2000)."

For example, a teenager may experiment with alcohol, even though he may have a close relative who is an alcoholic, because he believes he has the power to resist the addictive temptation.

From the report Raising Teens: A Synthesis of Research and a Foundation for Action, they offer five basics to parenting adolescents:
- *Love and Connect*: Teens need parents to develop and maintain a relationship with them that offers support and acceptance, while accommodating and affirming the teen's increasing maturity.
- *Monitor and Observe*: Teens need parents to be aware of—and let teens know they are aware of—their activities, including school performance, work experiences, after-school activities, peer relationships, adult relationships, and recreation, through a process that increasingly involves less direct supervision and more communication, observation, and networking with other adults.
- *Guide and Limit*: Teens need parents to uphold a clear but evolving set of boundaries, maintaining important family rules and values, but also encouraging increased competence and maturity.
- *Model and Consult*: Teens need parents to provide ongoing information and support around decision making, values, skills, goals, and interpreting and navigating the larger world, teaching by example and ongoing dialogue.
- *Provide and Advocate*: Teens need parents to make available not only adequate nutrition, clothing, shelter, and health care, but also a supportive home environment and a network of caring adults.

Identifying temptation can be difficult, and even as adults we may have trouble navigating through the things that could potentially harm us. However, if parents prepare their children with the tools they need to make wise decisions, then children will be more successful in making right choices.

We often teach our children lessons we would like for them to learn from our childhood, in hopes of helping them avoid making the same mistakes. Talking with your children about relevant situations that you encountered while growing up, will give them a reference point by which to measure the choices they make. Self-help author and motivational speaker Brian Tracy, separates choices into four categories. "Command decisions which can only be made by you as "The Commander in Chief". Secondly, Delegated decisions which can be made by anyone, such as the *color of the bike shed*, and should be delegated, as the decision must be made but the choice is inconsequential. Third, Avoided decisions, where the outcome could be so severe that the choice should not be made, as the consequences can not be recovered if the wrong choice is made. This will most likely result in negative actions, such as death. Finally, "No-brainer" decisions, where the choice is so obvious that only one choice can be made." However avoided and no-brainer decisions have been combined to form a collaborative decision, where consultation is needed and the decision is in agreement with others. Ultimately, what your children needs to know is that even if they may not like the choices presented to them, they have options. If we take the time to view our own options before making our choices, then our children will see this. And this, in turn, could help them keep from making decisions while in an emotional state. I've learned throughout my own experiences that if I stop and think about my options, I am arming myself with the tools to make the right choice for me.

As children recognize they are making the right choices it becomes instinctive. Before they reach this point though, it's only natural that they make some wrong choices along the way. Temptation is encountered by everyone, at various points in their lives. And, curiosity is a common trait of children. So, from a child's perspective, "Even when I make the wrong choices, will you still love me for me?"

Curiosity is a healthy trait but if not managed appropriately, it can lead to unfortunate outcomes.

CHAPTER ELEVEN
LOVE ME FOR ME

"As a teenager I was so insecure. I was the type of guy that never fitted in because he never dared to choose. I was convinced I had absolutely no talent at all. For nothing. And that thought took away all my ambition too."~ Johnny Depp

A teenager trying to find his own identity, making "the right" decisions became more difficult than I could imagine. Before then, it was my mother making most of my decisions coupled with being educated in a private school. My environment was unusually controlled. For so long my mom and others were telling me what to do. I was tired of it; I wanted to make my own decisions. I was raised with the understanding school was for learning. "Why do you feel the need to misbehave and not follow directions?" my mother would ask, if she was informed that I misbehaved in school. "Have you forgotten what school is meant for?" I guess I had... for my view of school started changing.

Now as an adult I understand why I had those difficulties... sometimes I was bored, distracted by friends, or I simply didn't understand the subject matter being taught. I think back...Why I did not speak up to tell my mother and explain what I faced as a teenager?

I wished I would have done so. One of the big changes in my life was when Erinn and I were transferred to public school. It was an entirely different world. Transitioning was difficult as we had no idea of what to expect. Between the stories we heard from people in our neighborhood who attended and the images portrayed by the media. The environment did not appear to be one in which we were accustomed.

Wearing a uniform to school is what Erinn and I was used to. It had become part of our routine... an orchestrated functioning each day. Wearing clothes to make a fashion statement felt like a daily popularity contest... which was a completely new concept for us. Some students considered our attire to be a bit preppy. They appeared to think we thought of ourselves better than them, transferring from private school which they associated with being very smart and rich. What they did not understand was we were just teenagers like them.

I remember this boy had stolen my brown leather jacket from my locker, one of the first weeks I was there. I did not know how to react. This had never happened to me before at school... a place where I am supposed to be safe. Then a few days later, I found it -- on someone else that is – and confronted him, "Eh, that's my jacket!" But, he replied, "No, it's not, my mom bought this jacket." Fighting was not an option... knowing this was unacceptable to my mother. And, there was no way I wanted to end up in the principal's office! Later that evening, I told my mom that I had found my jacket and had confronted the kid. She asked, "Well where is it?" I responded, "He said his mother bought it for him. I know you would not want me fighting in school…Right?" The next day she went to the school and spoke to Mr. Jones, the principal. Mr. Jones called the boy's mother who had no idea that her son was accused of stealing my jacket. She apologized for the incident and instructed her son to return the jacket the following day. Reflecting on the way I handled the situation, the lessons learned from that fight I had in elementary really came through for me.

My mother, viewed as middle class, worked long hours, but sacrificed in areas she thought necessary... just as her parents did. Erinn and I were average students, but excelled with our natural talents. My friends, students in the accelerated science courses, dressed and talked like I did. It was not intentional, just instinctive. However, once in these courses, I still found myself trying to fit in. Going through so many changes at once – physically, emotionally, and a new school, I felt confused.

As a teenager in high school, the pressures of being accepted among friends and peers were overwhelming. The talk of sex seemed to echo around me. My desire and physical attraction for beautiful women felt uncontrollable. There was nothing special about my physique... since I wore glasses, was short, and had a mouth full of metal. This made me feel like an outcast during my early years of high school. The popular guys were tall, athletic, and handsome... attributes most guys envied and craved to possess. Viewed mostly by girls as their friend, it humbled me. This, along with growing up in a house with two women, I had no choice but to learn to respect them. Watching how a man who dates my mother would treat her... and seeing boys lust over my sister, allowed me to take a front row seat to see how guys treated women. Some of those exchanges where pleasant, others not so much. Instantly my chivalry kicked in...wanting to make sure they were protected and always felt safe.

During the summer leading into the tenth grade my body started changing. I grew taller and more confident as I continued playing sports. Girls began taking notice and flirting with me --- thoughts of sex began running through my mind. I rarely hung out with my peers, because there were times I struggled with being myself around people. I resorted to humor to take the edge off. I did have two close buddies -- Carlos and Ryan my closest friends....polar opposites. Carlos, the Rico Suave of the group – would give his girlfriend's floral arrangements in vases. He had pretty easy access to all sorts of flowers because his father was a florist. I envied him and his ability to lure any beautiful girl in school. Ryan, on the other hand, was the ultimate athlete. The star of the show on any athletic platform, he was loved by women as well. How could I compete with these guys? I didn't really need to; since they were my friends. But, I do admit telling myself, "Man I got to get it together." I had no idea how to talk to girls and less about being a boyfriend... forget about taking it to the next step. I learned from what I saw on TV and what my friends were doing. My older cousin Dawn, who I considered my "big sis," would let me drive her car and give me pointers on what to do to help me become popular. She would introduce me to her college friends. In total awe of the beautiful ladies who thought "I was cute," If I may say so myself, I had definitely made progress in my sex appeal. Her best friend persisted with asking me of my first sexual experience. Of course, I lied and told her I had lost my virginity in the 9th grade. She must have known from my body language that I was being dishonest. But, lying relieved the stress of having to deal with the constant "who, where, and how it happened". I could not tell if she wanted to be my first lover or if she in fact was attracted to me. Regardless, she was "hot" and I knew she had a line of guys wanting to be with her. I finally came clean about my virginity on my Aunt Mary's back porch. So, we started talking about how we would end this so-called torture for me emotionally and physically -- I just wanted to get it over with.

During a trip to Texas, Kim and I planned to take this step, while visiting family in Houston. And while they were attending my younger cousin's football game, we locked ourselves in my Aunt Bridget's bathroom and had sex. When we were done, I honestly felt like I had given my heart away. Nonetheless, I had a story to tell my friends... sex with a college woman was a huge deal.

Time passed Carlos, Ryan, and I transferred to public school the following year. By this time, I had several girlfriends and even invited a few to meet my mother. They certainly were an assortment of characters. I remember one girl being so superficial. "Do you like my hair?" she would always ask. My mother and sister still give me a hard time about her. From the studious to the clueless, each were cute in their own way. Because of this, my humbleness began turning into cockiness and borderline disrespect -- using girls for temporary pleasure. Where along the path did I lose my way? "I'm not taking care of any babies," My mother would say, while conversations with my Uncle Lee would start with "Do you want me to build you a condom? I have some extra wood in the back." I did not feel attached to any of these women until I met Adrianne. Now she was the total package... smart, athletic, and curved like a sculpture of a goddess.

Adrianne appeared impossible to impress…..How could I compete? She dated a college guy who drove a red 1993 Mustang Cobra. I had no chance…so I thought. We had English class together, I stared from behind in a daze, not paying any attention to the lessons the teacher lectured on. So, one day I gathered the nerve to say something to her. I remember it happening all over again…words fumbling out of my mouth -- she must have thought I had some sort of speech impediment. She smiled and walked away. That night I practiced what I would say to make up for the blunder. The next day I approached her again... this time asking for her help with my English class work. I was so mesmerized; I did not know what to say. Weeks went by and she helped me with my English homework, as I helped consoled her with her problems at home. For that first year we became really good friends. My senior year, she started having problems with her boyfriend. Being a friend I gave her advice, along with giving her a young man's perspective. She dated this guy off and on for the next couple of months. One day she came up to me in the hallway saying "Chris, I'm done!" Inside my body, my hormones were throwing a party, because I knew now I had a chance. Still, I comforted, "Adrianne, It will be O.K." I said. She would call to talk, and then I

My Child

finally asked her to go out with me. "No," she said at first...only later to change her mind.

    We began dating shortly after, and on one hot Saturday evening we planned to go to the movies. I put on my new Polo and Girbaud jeans with a hint of my favorite cologne "Cool Water." I drove to her house expecting to say hello to her family as I always did, but this time was different. As I entered in the house I heard yelling. Walking further in, it became louder. Adrianne told me "Chris, you have to take me and my sisters to my Aunt's house." I asked "Why?" She said "I'll tell you later, let's go!" As I see her two sisters come out, I see her father screaming at her mother coming down the hall. I don't know why I wasn't erratic. I simply asked him, "Is everything alright, Sir?" He slurred some words and I couldn't tell if he was drunk or what was wrong with him. Next thing I know he picks up a knife and tells me *"Get out of my fuckin house."* I replied *"Not until Adrianne, her mom and the girls are in the truck with me."* He began to charge at me. We tussled with the knife until I banged it out of his hand. Then we wrestled on the floor for what felt to be an eternity. Realizing he had no chance, he then began to cry. Not knowing how to respond... first, this guy is screaming and trying to kill me, now he's crying in my arms... I gently picked him up and told him, *"Everything will be fine; you just need some time alone."* As we all walked out of the house calmness filled the air. Adrianne held me tight as we walked to the truck. No words needed. Her family's faces expressed all the gratitude I needed. Adrianne, her mom and sisters piled into my GMC 1500 single cab truck and I drove them to her Aunt's. What a night!!

    Prom eventually came around. We were excited to be finishing high school, but dreading the both us attending different universities. We had become so close over the last two years; I did not want it to end. My mother let me use her champagne Chevrolet Lumina for the big dance. I cleaned that car better than any detail shop could have ever done. I drove to Adrianne's house, and as she opened the door, she looked absolutely gorgeous... with the most beautiful gown I had ever seen. I placed the corsage on her arm, thanked her mom and left. I felt like we were the only couple at prom.

She held me tight as I did her. It was here I realized I would always care for her. She knew me, while I knew her. Most importantly though, she definitely loved me for me.

CHAPTER TWELVE
LOVE. FAITH. HOPE.

"We will have to repent in this generation not merely for the hateful words and actions of bad people but for the appalling silence of the good people." ~ Dr. Martin Luther King Jr.

  Religion stood as one of the most valued pieces of my family's puzzle, but one I have difficulty processing even today. My individual curiosity started long ago with questions from "Why is the pastor talking for so long? Why can't I understand what he is talking about?" In our minds, we couldn't conceive why people are so emotional at church. My memory recalls Sunday mornings my mother calling out, "Wake up, it's time for church." I would reply "Man, it's the weekend" underneath my breath. I dreaded putting on slacks, a shirt, and a tie, how I hated wearing ties during those treacherous summer months. I would sweat just thinking about walking outside in long sleeves. My grandmother always believed "You need to look your best, when you enter the house of the Lord." I heard her, yet I still hated being uncomfortable. My entire family wore their best hats, dresses, and suits. My sister would have on her dress with ruffle socks and patent leather shoes. Oh how funny to see her get her hair combed, she would cry and fuss. With us all leaving my grandmother's house, we traveled down a paved road that side winded through turns and curves. That later transformed into gravel, throwing up dust along with rocks. "Why have I washed the car on Saturday, if it's going to get dusty on Sunday?" I wondered and never understood.

When we arrived at church, my cousins and I would play little games of kicking makeshift footballs through our finger goal posts. My family would constantly tell us, "Quiet down, pay attention," but the only thing we saw was an old guy talking about the same thing over and over.

The emotions people showed at church were what continued to puzzle me; crying then rejoicing then pleading for help, I kept thinking *"the pastor is only speaking--so, why all the drama?"* We would listen temporarily, and then talk about what we would play at home. "When we get home let's ride the bikes or make cabins out of the tin that was left over from the roof. No, I know, Black Belt Theater." We hated church. It was boring to us kids. Years went by; I always saw my family praying for one thing or another... constantly reinforcing to us that we should be grateful for the things we had; telling us "There are so many people in this world without, be grateful for what you do have." I heard, listened, and began to see. My social consciousness became evident; I would help people as much as I could. From volunteering to giving advice to kids my age (even though I was learning myself), my life began changing.

Traveling down that dusty road on Sundays began to resemble my life. The journey of how dirty, bumpy, and uncomfortable it is. My life too was full of twists and turns. I had been thrown from left to right. In some way reflecting back, it prepared me to be able to withstand the bumps and bruises through my own personal up and downs. As I began to wonder more and more why there was such a disparity between people, questions began to arise again. "Why are hundreds of thousands of people dying and suffering?" "Why is there so much hunger, poverty, and disease?" "If there is a God, why doesn't he come save these people?" So I started to ask these questions to my grandmother and she would say "The Lord has not gotten to them yet." That answer did not sit well with me, why did some people have to wait in line, when others were living well – "The Haves and the Have-nots" So, then I would ask my mother, and she gave a little more clarity by telling me, "Some people just don't know how to change their lives." The thoughts continued to multiply! "Why are people not telling them?" We lived comfortable with limited resources, so why are people not changing. Why hasn't God gotten to them yet? Why were there so many hungry children? Why were there mass genocides? The questions kept coming. I don't know if she was tired of the questions or did not know the answer. Her comment would be "Don't question God!" But, I felt I had to. I was always told, "We are all God's children." So, why did it appear he had favorites? I really wanted answers.

Even though I did not have the answers I wanted or needed, I still felt my life had purpose. There was something I had to do; I just didn't know what it was. Believing that my life would never be in vain, I set out to do the best I could. The love my family, friends, and people along the way gave me the desire to spread the same love and kindness to others.

By the time I turned twelve it became time for me to be baptized. My belief in God was minimal; I continued to hear about Him never seeing his presence. We attended classes to prepare for our baptisms. We read the bible, prayed, but it all seemed pointless. Until one day I was alone on my grandmother's steps. It was sunny as most summer days. I looked up to the sky and asked God "If you exist please show me a sign." I was desperate to believe. Within a few minutes of placing my heads between my hands, it began to sprinkle with drops of rain. He had made His presence to me. I "believed!" I went to tell my mother I was ready to take on the journey of accepting God.

The following Sunday we went down that same gravel road but an unexpected turn led to a destination known for our fishing not church. We were at a river that my uncles had taken me to fish. I had only ever known white perch, buffalo, crappies, and garfish to live there...not God. But on this day, I knew there would be no "fishing" today. *"Why are we here?"* I asked my mom. She said to be baptized. I replied. *"In a river." "What the?"* We all got out of the car putting on white robes. My cousin, Micaela, looked as puzzled as I did. We watched as the minister walked into the river along with the rest of the adults who were there. My cousin and I were instructed to enter the water; it felt odd walking into a river with fish, alligators and other unseen creatures to be "baptized". The minister started his ceremony of songs along with scriptures, and then asked if I had found "God." I had, but my mind focused on *"What is he about to do?"* There were other kids before me; he had placed his hand on their forehead saying a few words, then leaning them back, he placed their entire body under the water. "Now it's my turn." My heart was pounding. The only thing I could think about was holding my breath. Before I knew it, underwater I went. No warning. He brought me up, soaked from river water. The significance of the body being cleansed was the only reason, I could see.

My family dried us off, telling us "Now you are responsible for everything you do." We were of age where we needed to think of our actions before flying off the handle. The days of being in church being pinched for talking through sermons, laughing because the choir was singing off key was a "thing of the past". My mother did not care if the minister preached too long or the choir sang off key. She wanted us to respect their efforts, to give ourselves food for our heart and soul. As an adult I view religion differently because I continue to see the division among people. I view religion as rules to live by, for the benefit of the greater good--not to divide and conquer. Every day I turn on the television or hear news of extremists, priests and other messengers of the gospel, taking advantage of people who commit and depend upon a higher being. So often we place all our hope into the messengers who are humans that become weak as the rest of us. But, along with every other aspect in life, we have to find out the real truth for ourselves. People's spirituality and religion, their personal connection with God and the world, should be respected by all.

"Everything happens for a reason" is a phrase we hear all the time. *Why do things happen to me? Why can't I ever get out of the storm?* My Aunt Hazel use to tell me, "Everyone has problems, trouble doesn't last always." "We all will have our seasons of good and bad, but don't give up." The faith I had in myself was evident. So many times I wanted to give up, but seeing the battles my family encountered, there was no way I could give up. No way could I be the man that I am today.... I must instill these same teachings to my son. But the question of *"Why doesn't God come save his people?"* still eludes me. In my journey through life my heart has felt sorrow, happiness, and anger towards the unpredictability of the world. My inner strength helped me to persevere, regardless of what I thought I couldn't handle.

The definition of religion and the constant argument of who is correct continue to make it harder to accept. Religions for centuries have been the reasons for war, bigotry, discrimination, as well as a source of comfort, advice and a community of help. My personal connections to "God" started in my heart, never stepping on people's toes being judgmental, their beliefs and traditions are their own to hold. What makes anyone right to tell them who they are in their beliefs? As science tries to find proof of the existence of "God" we can only make our own judgments. Spirituality is finding the truth about oneself. What is your purpose? The decision is yours and yours alone. The way we see change may be good for us, but not so good for others, so we have to respect that. Our moral compass is navigated by our own interpretation.

THE QUESTION *"Why doesn't God save his people?"* My answer to this question was found through writing this book. In that God has already saved them all. Events that seem to be unforgiving, makes people react in ways to change and prevent events from happening again. We see it as advancement in technology, but it's simply his way of all people to find their purpose. Everyone has a purpose, but sometimes we don't see the signs, the opportunities. For a fear of failure or change, some people stay complacent. My son "Sloan", Erinn's Heart, all my family and friends, the encounters, conversations, highs and lows have constructed the "perfect storm". The storm of my life's work to share with my son to make him the man my family helped to make me.

Love unconditionally. Keep the faith. Hope for the best. But for any reason it doesn't work out, endurance is built along the way just as a badge of honor. Be excited for your child's future knowing you have done everything within your ability to place them in the best position to lay their own path to their desired success. That whatever turmoil they face in life will give them the power to continue in the journey of finding their meaning in life. Witnessing the events of others and the sacrifices to provide an easier pathway keeps them "keeping on." The constant battle of exclusion from society is a fear of many. The journey of life starts with parents preparing them to feel self-worth, living among strangers while making an impact on this world to make it a better place. Love has been taught in every aspect of life. First, in order for life to have meaning one has to love oneself then apply that same love to the children they bring into this world. Sometimes we feel the best we give is not good enough. We must take one step, one day at a time.

    Children are lost in this world without the guidance, knowledge and structure that gives them the correct view of the world. As I write this book I think about never actually being educated as a writer, only the drive to give information for the betterment of our children. I felt it was part of my life's work... I always thought my life was bigger than me, never truly understand what it meant. I just knew I had purpose. The journey of my life had joys and pains, making the "perfect me". My message to all parents is to give your child a fighting chance at this world opportunities and accepting whatever they choose it to be. As a parent we never want to look back and say "if I would have done this different they would have become……..." Only at the end of the day, "I prepared them to the best of my ability, but I was always resourceful in finding the true answer to life's questions". Never think you are prepared, because life will take you left when you were preparing to turn right. Approach each day with true effort and application, some days will be better than others. But, at the end of the day you want to say "I tried my best" and that is all you can ask from your children is to try their best. Never wonder what could have or should have been. Put everything on the line. There will be times when you feel like you have lost hope. But, step away sometimes, because so often the best teachers are patience and experience. There are always three sides to a story. The good, the bad, and the truth. Once the first two are heard, form your own conclusion. First, we must ask the question "What do I want for my child's life?", "Am I willing to sacrifice my pleasures and time to give my child the best skills to face the challenges of this world." Hopefully, it's not just the basics of health, education and diversity. But, what are my specific goals, my plan of action to accomplish it? Merely placing them in a good environment hoping they will prosper will not work. Like a garden, just because you plant the seed in the ground doesn't mean it will be fruitful. We have to make sure that soil is rich in nutrients as children in varied environments. Those seeds need water, not always relying on teachers, family and others to water it. Just as lack of rain is a defining characteristic of drought, lack of parental dedication is a defining characteristic of underdeveloped children.

  As parents, we must not forget our own flaws. Don't become complacent with undesired results, it's "who we are." Those flaws help mold us into our "perfect me". For this reason, there will be difficulty in following through on instructions for our kids, stay focused. Our children are already overwhelmed with endless information, but without a buffer to interject and promote, it will be difficult. The role as a parent is truly the hardest, being placed on a pedestal of constant watch by our children. The task is difficult, everyone has their vices, but as we try to refrain from displaying it in front of our children. It helps us to face some of those weaknesses we have been challenged with.

  The society we live in feels like there is too much emphasis placed on achievement in young children. Every child performs differently, but the key is to find out what they truly enjoy and hold them accountable, but giving effort to all tasks regardless of likes or dislikes. Performance has been assessed by on demand results. Not taking in the variables that influence each child. Children have ability to excel at any subject, the only difference is the skill that has not been mastered. In saying every child has his own strengths and weaknesses, this statement is true. But the phrase "I'm not good at …" Whatever it may be, from math to science to writing. That statement only relinquishes them of the responsibility of becoming better at it. There are some things children find less interesting. It is not because they are boring, but it may be presented initially as bland or dull....as young children view vegetables. No matter how credible information is, if people are not interested in it, then it is useless. Continue to have your own personal standards for achieving. Don't have them dwindle only because your child grows older. Some children can become self-reliant through everyday interactions with life; but some children need constant monitoring to keep order.

As parents we all feel like we have failed at times, but it is not that you have failed, just more work to do. We want children to be able to face the world with no fear, no hindrance to try anything. We want them not to be victim of any environmental situation. The moment we feel like all hope is gone, go to your support if it is God, inner strength, or family. Just let go of the worry, fear and allow higher power to do as it must. The imprint we leave on our children as they go out on their own should be one of your life's lessons and journeys to be used as reference. We endure with them so they may reflect upon. In raising your child you can only set the foundations you make yourself aware of. But as they mature and make choices, you must have faith and hope that their decision making is not abrupt and impulsive. Once they make those choices, choose carefully your behavior and words of encouragement. Focus on how to correct and move forward, that they find self-discipline next time. We ultimately want our children to be better off than we were. We work countless hours every day and feel there is never enough time. Don't worry... Our children will go on to be great people, but will they look back and wonder if I was given the opportunity would I have been in a better position? In my journey through life do I yearn for a dream or goal? Do I have the tools to draw the blueprint of my passions? As a parent we want to make sure they get a fair chance. The feeling should be "I did everything possible to control the influences and experiences."

We take for granted the simplest forms of life…. air to breathe, food to eat, because luxuries have always been within reach, but it hasn't always been like that. Our ancestors, no matter what race, have sacrificed the ultimate price, so that we may have these opportunities. Sometimes, we focus on what we don't have instead of what we do have. Strip away grocery stores, *"How do you cultivate food to eat?"* Strip away clothes, *"What will we wear to cover us?"* Strip away structure, *"Will people respect each other?"* We are often reminded, what it means to truly live, especially when natural or man-made disasters occur. We all witnessed the events of 9/11, the reasons behind it along with the response of people, not just in America but across the world. Emigrants that come to America from vast lands of little or no resources maximize all the resources we provide. Coming from nothing and given access to everything, a notion we all should think about. Be resourceful. We live in a time where access to information is everywhere on the Internet and the access to the Internet is on almost every piece of technology. There are multiple organizations that have free access from health tips to cultural exposure to everyday questions. Find ways to incorporate the balance in your child's life to help to attain their definition of success and happiness.

"Teaching a child what you know is culture, educating that culture is parenting"~ C.S. Harrison

ACKNOWLEDGEMENTS

MY CHILD grew from days of constantly giving advice to parents at Erinn's Heart Early Learning Academy. Once my son was born, I asked myself if I would be able to live up to the standards that I set for other parents. I told myself I would, but I only knew about the first five years of a child's development. That is when *MY CHILD* took on a life of its own. After finding information for myself, I felt inspired to share this information with everyone. This journey could not have been completed without GOD who allowed my mother and father to conceive me. Shirley and Henry Harrison have always encouraged me to take control of my life. My wife Tina, who continues to support me when it seemed as if I was going insane, and Erinn who took me on her journey of starting Erinn's Heart Early Learning Academy. This book allowed me to face my fears and release my insecurities. I am continuously inspired by all of my family, friends, and people I have met along the way, who have shared information to improve my outlook on the world.

REFERENCES

- National Research Council and Institute of Medicine, From Neurons to Neighborhoods: The Science of Early Childhood Development, ISBN: 0-309-50488-0 (2000).
- www.developingchild.harvard.edu
- "Gaining Control of Ourselves" George Anderson, Anderson & Anderson ISBN: 0-9743682-3-7 2005
- Peter Gray, The Decline of Play and the Rise of Psychopathology in Children and Adolescents, www.psychologytoday.com
- Randy Brown Ph.D, University of Nevada, Area Extension Specialist for Children, Youth and Family Team
- Ethic Alarms, Jack Marshall, www.ethicalarms.com
- Malcolm Gladwell, The Tipping Point (Little Brown, 2000)
- www.wikipedia.com
- www.EthnicMajority.com
- How to persuade the Lazy Person- Inspiration vs. Desperation, www.magneticpersuasion.com
- Claudia M. Mueller and Carol S. Dweck, Praise for Intelligence can undermine Children's Motivation and Performance, Journal of Personality and Social Psychology 1998, Vol 75, No1, 33-52
- Donald F. Roberts, Ph.D, Media and Youth: Access, Exposure, and Privatization, Journal of Adolescent Health, 2000, 27 S, 8-14
- Regional Educational Laboratory At Serve Center UNC, Greensboro, Reducing stereotype threat in classrooms: a review of social psychological intervention studies on improving the achievement of Black students, REL 2009 No 076
- www.changetheequation.org, Mississippi STEM vital signs
- www.forbes.com
- Karen Stephens, When Parents Disagree on how to Discipline, Parenting Exchange, Exchange Press 2003

- Ingrid M. Nembhard, Ph. D, When Do Organizations learn from each other? Interorganizational learning in Healthcare, Industries Studies 2008, http//webmit.edu/is08/program
- National US Department Center for Educational Statistics (2011)
- American Students Show Steady Progress, www2.ed.gov, US Department of Education
- Salman Khan, www.khanacademy.com
- Will Allen, www.growingpower.org
- Brian Tracy, Time Power, 2007, pg. 153, ISBN: 0-8144-7470-5
- Simpson, A. Rae (2001). *Raising Teens: A Synthesis of Research and a Foundation for Action.* Boston: Center for Health Communication, Harvard School of Public Health.
- All photos www.shutterstock.com

www.ingramcontent.com/pod-product-compliance
Lightning Source LLC
Chambersburg PA
CBHW042315150426
43201CB00001B/7